NO. 10. WINTER 1998

NEW DIRECTIONS FOR SCHOOL LEADERSHIP

# The Changing Relationship Between Principal and Superintendent

## Shifting Roles in an Era of Educational Reform

REBECCA VAN DER BOGERT
Winnetka Public Schools, Evanston, Illinois

EDITOR-IN-CHIEF


SHERYL BORIS-SCHACTER
Lesley College School of Education in Cambridge, Massachusetts

EDITOR

THE CHANGING RELATIONSHIP BETWEEN PRINCIPAL AND SUPERINTENDENT:
SHIFTING ROLES IN AN ERA OF EDUCATIONAL REFORM
*Sheryl Boris-Schacter* (ed.)
New Directions for School Leadership, No. 10, Winter 1998
*Rebecca van der Bogert*, Editor-in-Chief

Microfilm copies of issues and articles are available in 16mm and 35mm, as well as microfiche in 105mm, through University Microfilms Inc., 300 North Zeeb Road, Ann Arbor, Michigan 48106–1346.

ISSN 1089–5612    ISBN 0-7879-4275-8

NEW DIRECTIONS FOR SCHOOL LEADERSHIP is part of The Jossey-Bass Education Series and is published quarterly by Jossey-Bass Inc., Publishers, 350 Sansome Street, San Francisco, California 94104–1342.

SUBSCRIPTIONS: Please see Ordering Information at the back of the journal.

EDITORIAL CORRESPONDENCE should be sent to Rebecca van der Bogert, Winnetka Public Schools, 2759 Eastwood Avenue, Evanston, Illinois 60201.

Jossey-Bass Web address: www.josseybass.com

Printed in the United States of America on acid-free recycled paper containing 100 percent recovered waste paper, of which at least 20 percent is postconsumer waste.

# The International Network of Principals' Centers

The International Network of Principals' Centers sponsors *New Directions for School Leadership* as part of its commitment to strengthening leadership at the individual school level through professional development for leaders. The network has a membership of principals' centers, academics, and practitioners in the United States and overseas and is open to all groups and institutions committed to the growth of school leaders and the improvement of schools. The Network currently functions primarily as an information exchange and support system for member centers in their efforts to work directly with school leaders in their communities. Its office is in the Principals' Center at the Harvard Graduate School of Education.

The Network offers these services:

- The International Directory of Principals' Centers features member centers with contact persons, descriptions of center activities, program references, and evaluation instruments.
- The Annual Conversation takes place every spring, when members meet for seminars, workshops, speakers, and to initiate discussions that will continue throughout the year.
- *Newsnotes*, the Network's quarterly newsletter, informs members of programs, conferences, workshops, and special interest items.
- *Reflections*, the annual journal, includes articles by principals, staff developers, university educators, and principals' center staff members.

For further information, please contact:

International Network of Principals' Centers
Harvard Graduate School of Education
336 Gutman Library
Cambridge, MA 02138
(617) 495–9812

# Contents

*This chapter provides a window into how five pairs of superintendents and principals are thinking about their relationships. Here the volume editor explains the rationale for this issue's focus and contextualizes the discussion in the current conversation around educational reform and the schools of the future. As the locus of power shifts away from the central office and the tasks of the schools undergo redefinition, so must the relationship among the educational leaders.*

# 1

# Learning and communication as the linchpins for the superintendent-principal relationship

*Sheryl Boris-Schacter*

WE ARE AT A CROSSROADS in the history of our public schools, one that finds us struggling to fit a new vision into an old organizational structure. We are still working with the roles of educational leadership as they were defined decades ago and we are still driven by the original framework for what schools and school systems should look like and what each of the players should be responsible for doing. However, since the publication of *A Nation at Risk* in 1983, there has been a fundamental shift in the ways in which educators think about organizing schools as places for adults to work and for children to learn. The adults no longer are expected to go it alone,

NEW DIRECTIONS FOR SCHOOL LEADERSHIP, NO. 10, WINTER 1998 © JOSSEY-BASS PUBLISHERS

cherishing isolation and autonomy above collaboration and inter-disciplinary curriculum.

As the teachers have moved, albeit cautiously, outside of their classrooms and disciplines, they have had little choice but to notice issues regarding policy and practice that had previously been the purview of principals and superintendents. This new level of teacher awareness, along with reform initiatives such as whole school change, teacher leadership, and school site councils, have propelled teachers into new arenas. It is not unusual today, for instance, to find teachers involved in scheduling, budgeting, resource allocation, and grant writing. There is now a tacit agreement that gifted educators have a great deal to contribute to the educational enterprise outside the classroom and that it takes everyone's best effort to run a successful school.

An analogous blurring of traditional roles that has occurred concurrently and for similar reasons is that between the central office and school-based administrators. In many districts, site-based management has made principals more responsible for their school's performance, while the central office has backed further away from the day-to-day operations of individual buildings. It is reasonable to assume that if the expectations for administrators have changed, then the relationship between them must also have changed. It is the newly conceptualized relationship between principals and superintendents that provides the focus for this volume of New Directions for School Leadership.

In an attempt to illuminate how this relationship shapes the efficacy of schools, administrative pairs consisting of the superintendent and one principal from the same district were invited to prepare manuscripts. Contributors were instructed not to focus on the particulars of an individual but to reflect on the relationship generically, digging deeply into their own experience. Each was guided, but not limited, by the following questions:

- Given that school systems are loosely coupled organizations, how is the relationship between the superintendent and the principals managed?

- Are these relationships solidified or ruined by direct supervision?
- What matters most in these relationships? Is it size of the system, the gender and/or race of the parties, how much time is spent together, or personality?
- If school-based management is now prevalent, how might it tip the balance of power between the superintendent and the principals?
- The average tenure of a superintendent is less than that of principals. How might this affect the relationship between them? Does it mean that the principal is more likely to ignore directives and hope that he or she outlasts the superintendent?
- Is the school or the district the unit of reform, and to what extent is the relationship affected by the politics of the moment and its itinerant issues of accountability?

It was not entirely clear before the fact whether inviting teams of school leaders and publishing their responses back-to-back would aid our collective understanding of the superintendent-principal relationship. However, the informal feedback I received from writers indicated that most of them had engaged in discourse about the issues prior to their independent writing and that those conversations furthered their collaboration and nourished their determination. Evidence of these dialogues is dispersed throughout the contributions in the form of common language, shared sentiment, and similar analyses. The fact that the project itself became, in many instances, an intervention, justified the choice to invite leaders from the same districts separate from the question of whether patterns emerged from content. In fact, patterns did reveal themselves across districts. It became strikingly clear that it was the opinion of these school administrators that certain discernible attributes existed that characterized successful working relations between those who ran individual school buildings and those who ran whole school districts.

Although contributors used different words, there was a powerful reminder that the field of education is about pedagogy at every level of the organization. Many writers concluded that superintendents and principals are, at the heart of any thriving relationship, engaged in mutual teaching and learning. Meredith Howe Jones cautioned, however, that for a relationship of unequal formal power to encompass genuine mutuality it had to provide "reciprocal security." In other words, although we agree in theory that education is a lifelong process, we sometimes forget to forgive ourselves for not knowing everything. Greg Willis noted that when we feel safe enough to communicate honestly, we have the opportunity to "recognize passions and run with dreams." It is easy to imagine the ripple effects in school systems when the superintendent-principal association can be described by such dynamic terminology.

The other theme as ubiquitous as mutual learning was the centrality of communication, in all its manifestations. Mike Schwinden reminded us that the first step toward overcoming the inherent difficulties of having good communication in a physically scattered organization is simply "the resolve to communicate." Authors cited several pluses to the approach of greater disclosure, including the prevention of problem escalation, the avoidance of public surprises, the evolution of shared meaning, and the development of a culture of inquiry and professional reflection. Not surprisingly, it is but a small step from honest and frequent communication to mutual learning. What is also compelling here is that, in the aggregate, the chapters begin a conversation about relational communication regarding race and gender that bears continuous scrutiny as more women and people of color assume leadership roles in K–12 education. If communication is vital, then we must know how to do it effectively in spite of entrenched racism and patriarchy.

The authors of this volume of *New Directions for School Leadership* associated both mutual learning and open communication between the superintendent and the principal with systemic change and educational reform. They reasoned that when people in positions of power and leadership think deeply and genuinely together on issues salient to the schools, then these same people are willing to take the risks necessary to try new initiatives. The contributors grew to understand that authentic partnerships lessened territorialism and built collateral for celebrating future triumphs and weathering inevitable disappointments. This is the premise under which the volume began. I raised the question of whether the new expectations articulated under educational reform for greater collaboration between the central office administration and the building principals meant that these individuals would have to forge fresh models for working together. If the responses of these five leadership pairs is any indication, then the answer is "Yes."

## Reference

National Commission on Excellence in Education. *A Nation at Risk: The Imperative for Educational Reform.* Washington, D.C.: U.S. Government Printing Office, 1983.

SHERYL BORIS-SCHACTER *is an associate professor and director of the Educational Administration Program at Lesley College School of Education in Cambridge, Massachusetts.*

*This chapter focuses on the superintendent-principal relationship as a setting for mutual learning. The author discusses why such a relationship is important and what organizational contexts support it. She argues that the hallmarks of a successful relationship include the development of shared meaning, a culture of inquiry, reciprocal security, professional reflection, and respect for the reasons given by those who are resistant to change.*

# 2

# Building bedrock: The superintendent and the principal as mutual learners

*Meredith Howe Jones*

RELATIONSHIPS DO NOT just happen, they are made. They require hard work whether they involve a spouse, a friend, a colleague, or a subordinate. Given this reality, as a superintendent I know my work is cut out for me as I labor to develop relationships with a district's principals. My intent is to provide a setting where all parties—the superintendent and principals—can regularly examine existing ways of thought and behavior that govern their work. Within this context both can develop beneficial constructs and actions in the interest of furthering the district's goals. The assumption is that the principal will be able to transfer new ideas and behaviors to working with her staff. As the school district's leader, I must use my own experience and knowledge, combined with the authority of my

NEW DIRECTIONS FOR SCHOOL LEADERSHIP, NO. 10, WINTER 1998 © JOSSEY-BASS PUBLISHERS

position, to interact and produce "the consequences not of competition but of learning" (Jentz and Wofford, 1979, p. 9).

When I talk about learning in this context, I see it in two interrelated levels. One level is the type of learning that comes from exploring the assumptions that underpin our approach to teaching children, for example, those underlying ideas that shape our view of how children at different ages learn best, what should be taught and when, how parents should be included, and so forth. In this case, our beliefs drive decision making about such areas as the philosophy we look for in the teachers we hire, how the school is organized, the nature of the curriculum, and the instructional approaches we encourage. I call this level of learning "content learning."

The second level of learning is that which comes from looking closely at how we approach difficult interpersonal interactions. Such situations can range from how to deal with an angry parent, how to give constructive negative feedback to an underperforming teacher, and whether and how to counsel-out a mediocre long-tenured teacher. In cases such as these, if my relationship with a principal has developed to a high level of trust and if the principal is willing, in addition to using disciplined talk to explore the situation, we may add the technique of role playing an upcoming interaction to clarify the message, surface the principal's worst fears, and experiment with alternative approaches. This level of learning I call "personal learning." It requires inquiry into the fundamental beliefs and fears that drive our imaginings and ultimate responses to difficult interpersonal interactions. (For detailed case examples of principals who have developed new learnings in the latter realm, see Jentz and Wofford, 1979; Jones, 1982).

## Why an Emphasis on Learning

Schools, like any business, must regularly reevaluate the delivery of their core business techniques—in this case, teaching and learning—to be effective. New requirements for graduates entering higher education and the workplace, a plethora of state and federal mandates, reduced local control, an increasing diversity and number of students with special learning needs, greater parent involvement, and increased fiscal constraints, to name a few examples, mean that the environment of schools is constantly changing in both perception and in deed.

Such changes demand that schools probe old patterns of behavior and response and consider fresh ones calling out for new actions. The design of each school district's effort will vary within its own context. There is no end to this task, for it is not systematic and linear. The critical ingredient is that leaders must be learners, enabling them to open the school's culture to a continuum of learning for all, not just for students.

The repetitive nature of work can lead us to handle new events from the perspective of old unexamined assumptions. In discussing the work of practitioners, Donald Schön (1983) writes that the practitioner "is able to 'practice' his practice. He develops a repertoire of expectations, images, and techniques. He learns what to look for and how to respond to what he finds. As long as his practice is stable, in the sense that it brings him the same types of cases, he becomes less and less subject to surprise. His knowing-in-practice tends to become increasingly tacit, spontaneous, and automatic" (p. 60). Schön goes on to say:

As a practice becomes more repetitive and routine, and as knowing-in-practice becomes increasingly tacit and spontaneous, the practitioner may miss important opportunities to think about what he is doing. . . . And if he learns, as often happens, to be *selectively inattentive* to phenomena that do not fit the categories of his knowing-in-action, then he may suffer from boredom or "burnout" and afflict his clients with the consequences of his narrowness and rigidity [p. 61; emphasis added].

The main focus of a principal's work is to provide instructional leadership. In the service of this goal, each day he faces a breadth of tasks that would astound those unfamiliar with the role: he might meet with an inquiring parent, untangle a classroom scheduling problem, undertake a classroom observation, restrain an out-of-control student, meet with a teacher to discuss her performance, investigate a student theft, write a memo, and meet with a curriculum planning group. Each task requires an infinite number of minute decisions, many of which he is not even consciously aware. As he experiences numerous variations of repeated phenomenon, he develops a repertoire of strategies and techniques that become automatic but not necessarily appropriate. Without regular examination of this work, there is a real danger that the principal will respond to new situations in old ways. The constant application of preexisting frameworks can lead to narrowness and rigidity.

While principals and superintendents do reflect regularly on their practice, without determined disciplined inquiry, as Donald Schön suggests, each can easily get stuck in the web of her own routines and lack of thought. If the organization as a whole is to learn, its leaders must also be learners.

Research and practical experience join to indicate that schools rarely undergo substantive change without the leadership and support of the principal. Similarly, there are severe limitations to what can be accomplished by an individual teacher's effort unless the entire school culture is supportive and geared to the notion that adults must be learners.

In my view, when the superintendent-principal relationship is effective, they become partners in open reflection through thoughtful discussion about the norms and beliefs that govern action and how they might alter their behavior in the interest of improving teaching and learning. The ideal partnership is one in which each can question, reexamine, and reevaluate the other's norms and behaviors as well as his or her own. This is mutual learning at its best.

## Conditions for Mutual Learning

From my perspective, the superintendent's relationship with a school district's principals begins when the prospective superintendent has her first interview for the position. Impressions are formed; assumptions are made. When the superintendent is hired, how she begins will play a critical role in setting the stage for the nature of future relationships.

A change in organizational leadership is a "golden moment" that provides a unique opportunity for the school district to pause and take stock of itself. A carefully designed and public "entry plan" can capitalize on that moment through conversations at planned meetings between the superintendent and the major stakeholders— school board members, administrators, teachers, parents, and so on—to determine their perceptions of "what is" as well as their hopes and dreams for "what might be." Such activities, followed by a public sharing of the superintendent's view of the major "motifs" or themes expressed during these meetings, as well as any discrepant information between constituencies, not only brings to the surface important data but sends a powerful message at the start (Jentz, 1982). Simply stated, the message is: the superintendent values open inquiry with a focus on the district and with the goal of it becoming the best. Seeds are planted for building a culture of inquiry.

Equally important, the superintendent is laying a foundation for developing trust and is exhibiting behavior that will serve as bedrock for his relationship with principals over the long term. Through his entry conversations and subsequent presentation of findings back to stakeholders, he models values such as openness to inquiry and learning, thoughtful synthesis of information, and a willingness to test assumptions and explore alternative perspectives. These are the same qualities we search for in outstanding principals and teachers and in their classroom learning environment for students.

I think it important to point out that "entry" as I describe it here is vastly different from the traditional stance in which "entry" is conceived as "when I begin I will talk with key people." Unlike the latter approach, an entry plan is structured such that everyone knows the groups or individuals with whom the superintendent is meeting and when, what questions will be asked, followed by a public presentation of the superintendent's findings in order to test their validity.

As with her carefully designed architecture for entry, the superintendent, by virtue of the authority which comes with her position, is able to create the necessary structures for articulating the district's direction and engaging people in disciplined inquiry about norms and beliefs. Structure in this context includes such activities as establishing meeting times and frequency, setting agendas, and framing and managing the discussion within those agendas.

Regular contact with principals, individually and as a group, provides a crucial foundation for open inquiry. Regularly scheduled one-on-one meetings are essential to personal reflection beyond the eyes of colleagues. Exploration of thoughts and feelings can be deep. Interpersonal connection can be strengthened.

At the same time, districtwide administrative meetings create a context for group inquiry. The views of each individual are enriched by those of all. Together, the group can inquire into existing practice and its underlying assumptions, and invent new action around shared goals that link the past to the future. Robert Evans (1996) writes that "flexible, developmental planning and the building of shared meaning demands that leaders listen actively to staff, modify their initial goals to reflect staff experience, and aim toward building innovation that is truly collaborative wherever possible" (p. 18). By the same token, leaders must listen to each other in order to develop shared meaning and mutual plans to further districtwide and school-level goals.

Open inquiry is doomed unless the superintendent provides a nondefensive setting with each principal through caring and commitment, including acceptance of mistakes; offering comfort, support, and ideas; and, most important, demonstrating a willingness to question the superintendent's own dogma. As Jentz (personal communication) wisely noted to me, "You must give good data to get good data." The superintendent must be comfortable sharing his own norms and beliefs in order to check assumptions and explore discrepancies. Such behavior demonstrates an openness that signals an acceptance of others doing the same. As a consequence, principals are more likely to feel safe in giving honest information about their own thinking. Otherwise, the principal will be afraid to share dilemmas about both substance and emotion.

I hold the view that if the superintendent can develop a relationship with the district's principals that provides reciprocal security, then together they can safely explore each other's suppositions. This honesty facilitates ideas for charting a new course when old skills do not work or formerly successful practices are no longer successful. Change requires invention; invention requires risk; risk requires an open approach to learning.

## The Role of Personality

From my perspective, how each personality is organized is a major variable in the way the principal-superintendent relationship develops. I use the term "personality" with reservation because of its multilayered meaning. For the purpose of this discussion, I do not use the word to refer to the unique traits or characteristics each of us exhibits, such as whether we are outgoing or reserved, whether we keep a neat office or a messy one, and whether we enjoy playing squash or chess. I refer instead to the deeper aspects of self, to how we construct meaning, acknowledge and reveal our thoughts and feelings, and conceptualize our world. Given this view of personality, if the goal of the superintendent is to nurture a relationship with principals that is dependent on reflection and inquiry, each person's method will vary, making each relationship unique.

For example, when the behavior of a principal is governed by a paradigm of leadership that valorizes being right, being in control, being invulnerable, and being rational (Jentz and Wofford, 1979), while the superintendent acts from a view that effective leadership allows one to accept and feel ambiguity; sees conflict and resistance as expectable; searches for questions and answers through interaction with others; and tries to maximize the amount and kind of information that is shared, the relationship between the two can generate considerable conflict. In this kind of relationship, the superintendent risks appearing "weak" because from the principal's perspective effective leaders show no ambivalence—they must always be right and in control. Such a principal is reluctant to examine jointly her own thinking. As a consequence, the superintendent must focus patiently on "unfreezing" old beliefs and acknowledging their attendant loss, with the hope of moving toward a shared commitment to a new set of norms and beliefs.

In this situation, the conflict between the superintendent's conception of leadership and that of the principal may be so deep that progress is close to impossible. As the school district's leader, however, it is incumbent on the superintendent to persist: to figure out how to carve out a relationship that will further progress toward the district's goals. With principals who are already open to learning, the task is obviously less difficult.

## Personality as a Reflection of Gender

"Personality" as a function of gender also has an effect. There is general agreement emerging from research and subjective opinion that suggests that "there are important and probably qualitative differences between modal male and female minds and personalities" (Robbins, 1996, p. 112). In discussing concepts of "socio-centric" and "self-centric" personalities, Robbins suggests that the female ("socio-centric") personality tends to be "structured in terms of complex patterns or networks of interrelatedness or interdependency within entities larger than the individual person" (p. 159), while the male ("self-centric") personality tends to be structured "around a separate and autonomous self" (p. 160).

Having worked with both male and female principals, I have experienced, in a general way, these differences reflected in the way the sexes think about their work and their relatedness to others. While there are many exceptions, male principals are often more emotionally closed off than their female counterparts; they rely more on "hard data"; and they seem less willing to express uncertainty. In my experience as a female superintendent, my relationship with a principal who is also female often quickly evolves into one based on communal expressions of caring and the exploration of ideas and feelings. With male principals, I often find a refreshing clarity of expression, greater decisiveness, and constructive uses of mathematical analyses. Nonetheless, to hold hard and fast to these generalizations would be a major mistake—after all, as Robbins also notes, "all human beings are more similar than different" (p. 112).

## Resistance to Learning

Likewise, it is misleading to generalize about principals who show reluctance to pursue innovation. I find that superintendents often construe a principal's or teacher's apparent rigidity about how things should be done in a pejorative way, attributing it "to some kind of character flaw" (Evans, 1996, p. 92). Such principals appear to be unable to reflect upon or utilize new information as a resource for learning and appropriate change.

Another way to view people's resistance is as a reflection of their integrity (Jentz and Wofford, 1979). If a principal's internal construction of leadership has consistently worked in his school, his whole self is likely to be invested in thinking about and doing his job in a certain way. He becomes deeply committed to a set of values about what constitutes an effective school. When he acts from those beliefs, he is acting out of a sense of integrity, that is, he is demonstrating consistency between his values, his goals, and his behavior.

As Evans (1996) points out, we are all resistant to change, even those of us who consider ourselves change agents. If deep and lasting change is to occur, the principal, the superintendent, and the teachers must work hard to make a shift away from antiquated views to those more applicable to the present. They must become resisters themselves, working to sustain the new norms and beliefs that support the change. Otherwise, there will not be lasting change, change that is appropriate and effective within the educational context.

Another way to think about resistance is to acknowledge that characteristically people are more or less ambivalent about change. On the one hand, they enjoy the status quo; on the other, they espouse change. Change is a challenge to competence; it generates feelings of loss. Our reflex is often to resist change (Evans, 1996; Jentz and Wofford, 1979). The problem is confounded in districts that are considered high performing as measured by standardized tests and college acceptance rates. Often principals in such districts see no need to change, since they reason that the way things are have always bred success.

## Conclusion

I believe that in a superintendent's relationship with principals it is imperative that she consistently focus on exploratory walks along the paths of both of their minds. While "none of us can be fully in touch with the entire range of our knowledge, perception, feeling, and skill" (Evans, 1996, p. 193), we must apply consistent scrutiny to those aspects of mind and behavior that are accessible to us. Otherwise, school leadership cannot make appropriate choices related to programmatic changes. School leaders must understand as fully as possible the underlying ideas that govern current forms of their practice before they are able to expand their patterns of thought in such a way as to enable them to make informed choices about shifting away from ideas and practices that no longer work.

To create the context for such inquiry, the superintendent must demonstrate a willingness to learn himself, use his authority to structure appropriate meetings and dialogue, and remain sensitive to peoples' need for psychological safety. He must understand and appreciate the role of personality in his relationship with principals, accept the reality that conflict is inevitable, and respect the underlying reasons of those who resist change.

## References

Evans, R. *The Human Side of School Change: Reform, Resistance, and Real-Life Problems of Innovation.* San Francisco: Jossey-Bass, 1996.

Jentz, B. C., with Cheever, D. S., Fisher, S. B., Jones, M. H., Kelleher, P., and Wofford, J. W. *Entry: The Hiring, Start-up, and Supervision of Administrators.* New York: McGraw-Hill, 1982.

Jentz, B. C., and Wofford, J. W. *Leadership and Learning: Personal Change in a Professional Setting.* New York: McGraw-Hill, 1979.

Jones, M. H. "Supervision: The Giving and Receiving of Negative Information about School Performance." In B. C. Jentz and others, *Entry: The Hiring, Start-up, and Supervision of Administrators.* New York: McGraw-Hill, 1982.

Robbins, M. D. *Conceiving of Personality.* New Haven, Conn.: Yale University Press, 1996.

Schön, D. A. *The Reflective Practitioner.* New York: Basic Books, 1983.

MEREDITH HOWE JONES *is currently superintendent for the Menlo Park public schools in Menlo Park, California; she formerly held the position of school superintendent in Weston, Massachusetts.*

*The author suggests that we draw upon what we as educators know about what constitutes good teaching and apply it to the relationship between the superintendent and the principals in a school system. He argues that the superintendent should take the opportunities afforded through positional power to nurture the practice of principals.*

# 3

# Superintendents: Principals' teachers?

*Paul A. Naso*

IT MAY BE THAT we need to hear ourselves say it to actually believe it: we are essentially teachers. Whenever the opportunity presents itself, we—superintendents and principals—are quick to identify ourselves as teachers. When we want to establish that we have first-hand knowledge about curriculum and methods, we relate experiences from our days in our own classrooms. We insist on being thought of as instructional leaders rather than as managers or executives. We also hasten to tell people that we miss having our own classrooms or that we regret that our current responsibilities reduce the time available for us to have more direct contact with students. We have a great deal to say to parents, community members, and colleagues about our identities as teachers, but, interestingly, in much of what we say, our words are paradoxical. In some instances we announce that we are fundamentally teachers, and in others we fret that our administrative roles distance us from teaching. We

NEW DIRECTIONS FOR SCHOOL LEADERSHIP, NO. 10, WINTER 1998 © JOSSEY-BASS PUBLISHERS

declare our attachment to teaching, but we also imply that teaching is something others do with young people.

Teaching, understood in a more general sense, should remain an essential endeavor of superintendents and principals, pursued not only in our interactions with young people, but also in our relationships with our colleagues. We know that adults in schools and school systems learn a great deal from each other, but learning from colleagues is often regarded as incidental, unplanned, or nondeliberate, something that just arises spontaneously when two well-matched educators somehow manage to find each other. With the exception of practica, internships, mentoring assignments, inservice programs, and other formalized arrangements, we tend not to think of ourselves as serving as each other's teachers. In particular, we are not accustomed to the notion of superintendents functioning in a teacherlike manner with principals.

## *Multidimensional and Complex Relationships*

Perhaps this is because there are other dimensions to the relationship between superintendents and principals that are predominant in our minds. For instance, we both function as specific links in the school system chain of command, and as such we relate to each other and are viewed by others in hierarchical terms. Another familiar side to the superintendent-principal relationship concerns supervision and evaluation. We expect evaluation and supervision to result in learning, but learning is not their primary purpose. They are often driven by the superintendent's responsibilities to uphold predetermined standards of performance and to make decisions about contract renewal or professional advancement. In a third common conception of the superintendent-principal relationship the superintendent operates as the leader of the administrative team and principals as collaborative contributors to the team. This understanding of their relationship concentrates primarily on decision making and problem solving, with principals representing the needs and priorities of their respective schools and the superintendent forging from these different perspectives a consensus or a common direction. All of these dimensions do require some forms of teacherlike behavior on the part of superintendents (for example, leading discussions, framing good questions, responding to work), but the teacher-learner aspect of the superintendent-principal relationship does not easily remain in the front of our minds when we are involved in these other tasks that usually have immediate importance.

Another reason that we do not readily accept the idea of superintendents teaching principals may be that we are uneasy with certain negative images we associate with teaching. We may worry that this description of the relationship underscores the principal's subordinate role and presumes that the superintendent is more knowledgeable, more skillful, or more insightful than the principal. We also may fear that by stressing that superintendents and principals have a teacher-learner relationship we are giving superintendents license to scrutinize principals, issue frequent and heavy-handed corrections and criticisms, or practice other unwelcome, unhelpful, or intrusive behaviors.

The previous examples illustrate two critical points: (1) superintendents and principals must interact in a number of different ways to accomplish a wide range of tasks; and (2) there exist in all of these interactions many nuances that have to do with control and power. It is an extraordinary challenge, therefore, amid all these pressures, to act decisively on administrative matters, to interact humanely and without authoritarian overtones, and to cultivate significant and positive teacher-learner relationships between superintendents and principals. Despite all of these considerations that discourage us from thinking of superintendents as principals' teachers, there are reasons for them to make a conscious effort to assume those roles.

## *The Superintendent's Opportunities to Teach*

It appears wise, first of all, for superintendents to remain mindful of the opportunity they have to shape an environment for adult learning. They act on that opportunity most directly in their use of language and in the meaning they give to the words and actions of others. We expect superintendents, far more than any other elected or employed school official, to lead the community as well as the school system in its ongoing conversation about education. Superintendents articulate vision statements and deliver other messages about education to everyone from faculty to parent groups to realtors. This communication has many purposes, but certainly it is intended to inform, to inspire, and to elicit support. Principals, however, are a different audience. Superintendents have an opportunity with principals to draw special attention to choices about what gets talked about and how it gets talked about within the school system. They are in a position to help principals consider the qualities to strive for in the discourse about education and schools, and thereby help them and others make better sense of their collective efforts for students. Principals should be more than another audience for superintendents: principals should be students of superintendents' words and actions.

To some degree superintendents act on that potential in subtle, implicit ways. They can dare to open up for discussion matters that might otherwise seem irrelevant or off topic. They are, after all, gatekeepers when it comes to which concerns get admitted at administrative meetings and thereby receive official administrative thinking time. Superintendents, in other words, can be instrumental in helping principals make room for important but neglected questions, ideas, or feelings. Imagine superintendents and principals discussing which aspects of their work they find most engaging intellectually, or how to search for balance between personal and professional lives. These topics, although they are not likely to be pressing school system issues, do deserve a place in the superintendent-principal dialogue because devoting attention to them helps to humanize our efforts and bring perspective to an overwhelming and dilemma-ridden set of responsibilities.

There are also more explicit ways that superintendents, through their close attention to the uses of language and meaning, may extend what principals know and know how to do. Generally speaking, they can foster certain habits of thoughtfulness that sustain principals' preparedness for handling difficult situations. In particular, superintendents can think of themselves as models for (1) reinterpreting and reframing complicated problems; (2) creating, intentionally and at appropriate times, disequilibrium in how a principal or principals have come to understand an issue; and (3) resisting rigid or oversimplified representations of pedagogy or curriculum. Of course, they need to show these habits in use, not merely offer them as theoretical ideals.

These habits have a way of settling to the bottom of the repertoires that principals draw from in handling problems in their schools. For example, initiatives in schools such as new programs or innovative curricula sometimes take on a life of their own and make great sense to those who are involved in their creation but require an enormous leap of faith by those expected to participate. Principals want to honor enthusiasm and hard work, but they also want to avoid misunderstood or poorly received programs, and they certainly want to prevent outright disasters. Without access to their full repertoires, they may choose simply to stand aside and allow the disaster to happen or they may cancel the initiative and thus discard a great deal of hard work already completed. Superintendents who consistently demonstrate thoughtful habits also help to keep principals prepared to intervene effectively, and in turn promote the same thoughtfulness in teachers so that problems at all levels are more easily anticipated.

Another opportunity that superintendents have is to emphasize the implicit messages conveyed by the school system and, hopefully, the alignment of those messages with systemwide core values and shared beliefs regarding teaching and learning. In some instances the messages are not readily apparent because they are left unspoken. For example, there may be assumptions about intelligence underlying certain grouping practices or beliefs about community and school climate indicated by policies related to class size or whole school enrollments. Superintendents teach by keeping their ears tuned to language and commenting on the coherence, consistency, and credibility in what we say. For instance, superintendents can identify instances when language does or does not convey a sense of hope and high expectations for learning. Leon

Botstein (1997) has referred to this quality as the "language of optimism." Botstein argues that linguistic choices are powerful indicators of how we feel about all children's ability to learn.

## Agreeing to Be Taught

The responsibility for building and maintaining a teacher-learner relationship does not reside totally with the superintendent. This dimension of the relationship remains unrealized if the principal does not accept and trust the superintendent's motivations. In the most basic terms, the principal must agree to "let go" of some autonomy and yield to the guidance and direction offered by the superintendent. This willingness to yield involves a considerable risk, and it presumes an honorable commitment from the superintendent. This tension needs to be addressed. Perhaps it is best addressed by having the superintendent and principal or principals talk directly about their understanding of their teacher-learner pact.

David Hawkins (1973) is an exceptional resource for reaching such an understanding. In "What It Means to Teach" he builds his brilliant exploration of the teacher-learner relationship from the suggestion by John Dewey that the most significant measure of any human association is the extent to which individuals learn from that association, that is, its educative value. Hawkins explains that the teacher-learner relationship, "by its very nature, involves an offer of control by one individual over the functioning of another, who in accepting this offer, is tacitly assured that control will not be exploitative but will be used to enhance the competence and extend the independence of the one controlled" (p. 9).

## Teachers, Not "Used-to-Be Teachers"

The preceding discussion was cast according to the question of whether superintendents are principals' teachers. It is reasonable to expect, however, that the teacher-learner relationship between superintendent and principal can be reciprocal. This is especially true when, as is often the case, the superintendent encounters less familiar territory. Not all superintendents have been principals. Certainly, not all superintendents have had experience at both the elementary and the secondary levels. Thus every superintendent would be wise to acknowledge that there are circumstances when principals can guide their superintendent's learning.

Finally, it is reasonable to expect that much of the teacherlike actions that have been suggested for superintendents in their relationship with principals are just as applicable to principals in their relationships with teachers, or, for that matter, when interpreted in a general way, in any teacher-learner relationship. It is crucial, however, that we—superintendents and principals—consciously and deliberately pursue this relationship and develop these skills. We should tune in carefully to our own words when we express our reverence for teaching. Of course, we can long for our days as teachers of young people. But our understanding of ourselves as teachers must be more than a memory. We must understand ourselves as teachers in the present. We are not "used-to-be" teachers. We are teachers.

### References

Botstein, L. *Jefferson's Children: Education and the Promise of American Culture.* New York: Doubleday, 1997.
Hawkins, D. "What It Means to Teach." *Teachers College Record,* 1973, 75 (1), 7–16.

PAUL A. NASO *is principal of the Country Elementary School in Weston, Massachusetts.*

*This chapter describes the tension between central-office administrators and building-level administrators as they continuously renegotiate their roles in the context of school-based management. The author makes a case for open communication so that substantive dialogue can ensue and unpleasant surprises can be avoided.*

# 4

# Better decisions without the surprises: Communication as the key to the principal-superintendent relationship

*Lonnie Yingst*

THE GREAT FALLS, MONTANA, public schools serve a community with a population of 60,000, with approximately 12,500 students in grades K–12. The student population is 87 percent white, 9 percent Native American, and 4 percent other minorities. The community's economy could be best described as serving the needs of a large agricultural area supplemented by a U.S. Air Force base. The Air Force base supplies approximately 14 percent of the grade K–5 student population. As a result of the history and size of our school district, we are organized administratively so that the superintendent does not have direct supervision of principals. That responsibility is assigned to two assistant superintendents, one for grades K–5 and one for grades 6–12. In my role as assistant superintendent K–5, I

NEW DIRECTIONS FOR SCHOOL LEADERSHIP, NO. 10, WINTER 1998 © JOSSEY-BASS PUBLISHERS

directly supervise two teachers, two supervisors, and fifteen elementary principals, nine of whom are women and six of whom are men. The focus of this chapter is the effect of communication, decision making, and evaluation on the relationship between the assistant superintendent and the elementary principals.

## *Communication*

If the relationship between the assistant superintendent and the principal is to remain strong, then communication between the two must be reliable and effective. Factors such as method of communication, the need to know, how individual personalities are expressed, and the tension between how issues are designated either district-based or school-based are just a few examples of the complexities involved in the transmission between the assistant superintendent and the principals.

The basic form of communication for our group is a regular bimonthly administrative team meeting. Over the last eight years I have tried both weekly seventy-five-minute meetings characterized by short concise discussion and three- to four-hour, twice-a-month meetings characterized by more in-depth discussion. Predictably, those principals who prefer concise bottom-line answers like the shorter meetings whereas those principals who need more information, accompanied by discussion, prefer the longer bimonthly meetings. It is my observation that the shorter, more regular, weekly meetings meet the needs of a site-based model but do not contribute to the development of an administrative team. The longer, more comprehensive, bimonthly meeting does a better job of nourishing the team concept, especially if care is taken to make certain all opinions are heard and communication is two-way. The danger in this second type of meeting is that those principals who tend to have strong opinions can dominate the discussion. As a result, care must be taken to share "airtime" equitably and counterbalance these large group experiences with small group meetings.

Small-group meetings generally allow more interchange between the assistant superintendent and the individual principals. This facilitates the process of the assistant superintendent gaining a better understanding of each principal's opinions and thoughts. This improved understanding can contribute to a positive relationship between the assistant superintendent and the individual principal.

Communication is further enhanced by individual or one-on-one communication. This communication takes the form of formal regularly scheduled conferences to discuss individual goals as well as school and district issues. These meetings can do much to lead to a positive relationship between the assistant superintendent and the principal if the participants are able to be open and honest about the issues at hand. Of course, if participants are less than candid, the effect on the relationship can be negative.

At least as important as these formal means of communication is the use of informal communication such as phone calls, e-mail, memos, and face-to-face contact. This kind of communication generally takes place on an as-needed basis. The key is knowing when and what to communicate. As is true of systems across the country, the Great Falls public schools are currently attempting to strike a balance between central and site-based control. It used to be much clearer who had jurisdiction when, but those roles and obligations have blurred as school-based leaders have become more empowered to effect change without consulting the central office, and the central office administrators have spent more time enabling principals to make those decisions. Site-based decision making holds advantages for students because constituents are so close to the issues and the action. Central office advantages include economies of scale, consistency, and coordination. The appropriate use of these less formal communication methods is critical to the delicate balance between central and site-based decision making.

The determining factor in knowing what is appropriate to communicate is deciding when there exists a need to know. Many issues that need to be communicated are obvious, such as student safety issues or actions by employees against the law or school board policy. However, other issues are less obvious and often involve a balance between site and central control. For example, friction can arise when the principal believes that a certain decision is hers to make and that the assistant superintendent should support that decision regardless of his own opinions. Conversely, the assistant superintendent can believe that the decision should be made at the central level and that the principal should support that decision regardless of her own opinion. There are occasions when this is the case, but they are rare. In reality almost all significant decisions require extensive and honest conversation, often over a period of time, between the assistant superintendent and the principal. In the final analysis, I believe, too much communication is always better than too little. We need to work against the temptation to communicate less because of the ever increasing demands on administrator time. Communication is the area in which there is the greatest potential to strengthen or weaken the relationship between the assistant superintendent and the principal.

## Making Decisions

Decision making has an effect on the relationship between the assistant superintendent and the principal. Literally hundreds of decisions are made in a school district on a daily basis. Most of these decisions are routine, so routine that they are not noticed. But it only takes one contentious or significant decision to affect administrative relationships in either a positive or a negative manner. Who makes these decisions and how they are made often determines the difference between a positive or a negative effect on this relationship.

For many routine decisions it is often obvious who should make the decision. Issues that are clearly site-based, such as internal schedules, arrangements for assemblies, routine discipline issues, parent/PTA issues, and the like (the list is endless) are decisions best made at the site level under the direction of the principal.

The process of decision making is probably more important than who actually makes the final decision. The extent to which the principal involves staff in making decisions that affect them has a direct effect on school morale. This morale eventually affects the relationship between the assistant superintendent and the principal because a school's staff always expects the assistant superintendent to makes things "better" for them when they have disagreements with their principal.

Many decisions are made centrally, such as those concerning staffing, for example, the number of teachers assigned to a specific building, because this is dictated by a large central budget. Since the number of teachers assigned is generally controlled by student enrollment and budget constraints, most principals and other staff generally accept these kinds of decisions. But decisions regarding assignment of that staff are sometimes more contentious. Again, how these decisions are made are as important as the decisions themselves. Issues such as whether there are single-grade classrooms or multiage classrooms or which teacher teaches a particular grade level require input from the principal as well as from other staff. If all persons at the site level affected by the decision are given opportunities for input, then acceptance is generally better. Unfortunately, it is also true that in the end the decision maker often winds up with negative residue, regardless of the degree to which the process was inclusive.

In the Great Falls public schools we believe that a well-articulated and coordinated instructional program provides all our students with the best educational opportunities. Therefore these decisions are made in the central office. Most of the instructional decisions focus on curriculum and materials adoption. The board of trustees, based on recommendations from a broad-based committee composed of teachers, the public, and administrators, follows a four-stage process for materials adoption. It includes forming the committee and comparing what is with what should be, drafting and adopting a curriculum, selecting supporting textbooks and instructional materials, and implementing and assessing the new program. As you can see, the process involves all staff as well as the public in these decisions. The principals and assistant superintendent play no greater role in this process than other staff; the final decision rests with the curriculum committee and the board of trustees.

However, the principal and the assistant superintendent play a major role in the implementation of any new program. Implementation decisions defining the parameters of the program are made centrally, with decisions within these parameters being made at the building or classroom level. These decisions have great potential to affect the relationship between the assistant superintendent and the principal. As discussed earlier in the Communication section of this chapter, I believe that the relationship between the assistant superintendent and the principal is enhanced through a process that requires everyone to participate in a discussion that eventually leads to a decision. This takes significant time, but it is time well spent. If care is taken to follow this kind of process in making curriculum-implementation decisions that may prove to be difficult or affect many different groups of people, then we can minimize the potential harmful effect on the administrator-principal relationship.

## *Evaluation*

Evaluation may have the greatest potential to jeopardize the relationship between the principal and the assistant superintendent. With the current emphasis in education on accountability, the evaluation process increases in importance. As is typical of many school systems, the assistant superintendent is located in a different building from the principal, therefore making ongoing evaluation and meaningful data collection more challenging. In Great Falls we use a goal-setting and validation process in combination with a rating scale designed to be used with supervisors. A variety of methods are used to collect information to evaluate progress on goals and determine which statement and rating to assign to each scale.

The goal-setting and validation process is generally controlled by the principal. He or she determines his or her own goals within general parameters set by the assistant superintendent. The parameters consist of at least three goals, with a minimum of one being instructional in nature and one being managerial. The goals are first discussed early in the year at a goal-setting conference. A midyear conference is held to discuss progress on the goals and an end-of-the-year conference is held to discuss completion or non-completion of the goals. This process relies upon the principal to self-report his or her accomplishments as to goals and provide appropriate documentation. This part of the evaluation process is generally well received by principals and the assistant superintendent and generally results in very few challenges to their working relationship.

A supervision rating scale that is part of the evaluation process proves to be slightly less congenial. It is designed to assign a performance statement or rating to the principal's performance from a low of 1 to a high of 5 on twelve different scales. The scales are (1) Personnel Management, (2) Instructional Supervision, (3) Professionalism, (4) Public Relations, (5) Business Management, (6) School Climate, (7) Student Management, (8) Facility Management, (9) Curricular Leadership, (10) Evaluation Skills, (11) Delegation, and (12) Organization. When using this tool the evaluator has the option to adjust the statements as needed.

The difficulty with the scales is collecting information to make appropriate decisions as to which performance statements to use. I use a variety of methods, including conversations with the principal, Iowa Test of Basic Skills results, observing a principal-teacher clinical supervision conference, observing school programs, observing PTA and staff meetings, parent/public comments and phone calls, survey data, Status of Education report (year-end curriculum and miscellaneous data report), and any other device that may seem useful. Even with these data sources, it is still a difficult task because for a vast majority of time a principal's work is not directly observable. As such, much is based on perception and trust.

From the goal process and the supervisor rating scale I produce an evaluation narrative that becomes the official evaluation document for a principal. It is this document that has the greatest potential for altering the relationship between the assistant superintendent and the principal. There can be a negative effect if there is disagreement about a particular rating. Hopefully, through open and honest discussion, the disagreement can be worked out. If not, the relationship can become strained. If we expect principals to realistically evaluate teachers, then the assistant superintendent must realistically evaluate principals. It is one method to ensure improvement in classrooms for students. We must, therefore, take the risk.

## Conclusion

Over the twenty-two years that I have been an administrator, administrative relationships have changed significantly. When I began in school leadership it seemed that the superintendent and/or assistant superintendent acted, as was expected at the time, in a rather authoritarian manner. Generally, these often unilateral decisions were accepted by other administrators, staff, and the public. Administrators tended to support each other. Many decisions directly affecting individual buildings were made centrally. Over the years, we have evolved to a more site-based or collaborative approach to administering our schools. Today decisions are openly questioned by other administrators as well as by staff and the community. This creates much more potential for disagreement, although this more open questioning approach does have the potential to help us make better decisions for our students because of the broad base of input. It is critical that we strive to develop a strong, positive relationship between the assistant superintendent and the principal. This is important if we are to provide the best education for our students. The key to overcoming the negatives is to employ an open and honest communication approach and work toward establishing consensus on those issues that affect all of us. The principal should not surprise the assistant superintendent and the assistant superintendent should not surprise the principal.

LONNIE YINGST *is assistant superintendent for grades K–5 in the Great Falls, Montana, public school system.*

*The author of this chapter argues that systemic and personal change are more likely to occur for principals and superintendents when there is more frequent, open, and two-way communication; more collaborative decision making; and more honest evaluation. These conditions are described as being difficult to achieve because they are time-consuming and personally risky, but worth the effort.*

# 5

# A principal's perspective on administrative relationships

*Mike Schwinden*

NOT ALL RELATIONSHIPS are complicated! One recalls the gentleman who attributed the success of his fifty-year marriage to the following arrangement: "I made all the big decisions and my wife made all the little decisions. Of course, she got to decide which was which." And so it is with principals and their supervisors: who makes which decisions can be the defining factor in their relationship. However, this author will argue that communication is the critical element.

## Decision Making

Principals, by nature, want to make decisions. To the extent a principal trusts her own judgment, she is inclined to make her own decisions, independent from the central office. On the other hand,

NEW DIRECTIONS FOR SCHOOL LEADERSHIP, NO. 10, WINTER 1998 © JOSSEY-BASS PUBLISHERS

some principals want (perhaps need) help from their supervisor in order to arrive confidently at a decision. In the decision-making process, principals must also recognize that some issues are broader than building issues, that is, they hold implications for the entire district.

Today managing individual schools and whole districts is more difficult than it used to be. Bad administrative decisions cost more money, waste more time, and involve more people than ever before. Poor decisions grind away at a district's efficiency, morale, and public credibility. Even mediocre decisions, over time, are debilitating to a system: district employees begin to disregard the exhortations of leadership and turn to colleagues for guidance and support.

When there is disagreement between the superintendent and the principal on a particular issue, the question arises: Who will make a better decision, the superintendent or the principal? On minor issues, it probably makes no difference. On critical issues, until the principal and superintendent can agree on a course of action, any decision will likely be wrong. Increasingly, principals and superintendents acknowledge a need to pool their information and ideas, and to trust each other's judgment, in order to survive.

### Local Trends in Decision Making

There was a time in Great Falls, many retired principals recall euphorically, when principals were left alone in their buildings to do their own thing. These same principals describe an evolution that took place over several decades whereby central office expansions began to encroach on the freedom to exercise judgment at the site. The encroachment was driven by time pressures, personal motivations, state and federal rules and regulations, and other factors. There is evidence in this district, however, that the trend has shifted back to building-based decision making in some areas.

### Budgets

Ten years ago, a building's principal controlled a budget of less than $5,000—money primarily used to purchase paper and miscellaneous supplies. Today the same principal would control a budget of $30,000. The assistant superintendent formerly managed budgets for staff development, teacher travel, textbooks, workbooks, and library books. Today, these decisions are made by the staff, with leadership provided by the principal, in each building. For example, the principal and teachers have the option of eschewing the purchase of reading workbooks and purchasing additional computer technology instead.

One continuing fiscal responsibility of the assistant superintendent is to prevent overspent building budgets. He also monitors requisitions as a precaution against purchasing irregularities, for example, purchasing a carpet sweeper with instructional funds. Ordinarily, he simply reviews the requisitions and passes them on to the purchasing department.

## Curriculum

While curriculum adoption decisions are still made by the elected school board (with input from district committees), the responsibility for implementing the curriculum and assessing it rests largely with the building principal. After an initial adoption, the central office typically arranges a few hours of staff development with the new materials; however, after that, the principal must see to the curricular training needs of her staff. This is accomplished at staff meetings and through early dismissals of students to accommodate in-building training.

## Personnel

Most important personnel decisions in this district are made by principals. However, between initiating the action and making a final decision, the judicious principal has informed and involved his superintendent(s). A principal decides when a nontenured teacher should be nonrenewed. He decides when a weak teacher needs remediation. When a teaching vacancy occurs, the central office administrative team screens the applicants down to a manageable dozen or so and the principal decides which of these candidates to interview. The interview team includes the principal, the assistant superintendent, and appropriate teachers. Ordinarily, the principal's first choice is the teacher hired.

---

## Communication

For principals, the good news is that most superintendents have an office located some distance from their school. The bad news is that this distance can become a troublesome barrier for communication. Communication between the central office and the principal is important for several reasons: (1) the superintendent has a broader perspective than the principal does; (2) the superintendent has access to information that the principal does not have—at the same time, the principal has better knowledge of issues in his building; (3) the superintendent is responsible to a larger constituency than the principal, and therefore must be aware of important problems and actions throughout the district; and (4) neither administrator can make good decisions consistently without the counsel of the other.

How is effective communication between the principal and the superintendent established? Both sides must first share a resolve to communicate. Agreeing to keep the lines of communication open is the simplest commitment to state and the most difficult to put into practice. Consider close friends who, upon parting, exchange phone numbers as well as electronic and residential addresses with sincere and noble intentions of staying in touch. Few do. One reason for this is that friends have an equal responsibility to maintain contact, hence neither does.

Superintendents ought to have the motivation and responsibility for initiating communication with their principals. Their survival is usually more tenuous than that of principals'; therefore the principals' support is valuable, perhaps crucial, to them. Furthermore, supervisors are generally less anxious about contacting and disturbing subordinates than vice versa.

Yet superintendents (and assistant superintendents) rarely visit schools and infrequently consult principals. Instead, communication most often takes place at scheduled meetings in the central office or by phone after a problem has developed. One reason for this is time: it is more efficient to bring several principals to one location than for a central office administrator to visit many sites. Real (and perceived) shortage of time is also a factor in a superintendent's reluctance to call principals and discuss substantive issues.

There is an alternative: principals must initiate the communication with the superintendent. For their part, superintendents need only encourage this effort, or, at the very least, not discourage it. Principals are in a position to share information, or seek counsel, when a problem is young—before it is ripe with unpleasant implications and repercussions. In addition, principals, especially those long tenured in the same building, tend to become parochial in their vision and insular in their decision making. Their judgment improves as it factors in the perspective of a knowledgeable, fellow stakeholder from the central office. There is, then, a mutual benefit in open and regular communication.

### Local Trends in Communication

There are fifteen elementary schools, each with one principal, in this district. For many decades the superintendent has had either one or two assistant superintendents who functioned as an intermediate administrative level between himself and the building principals. Today, the elementary principals report to, and are supervised by, the assistant superintendent for K–5 schools. The potential for access to the assistant superintendent is greater now than it was when one assistant was responsible for both middle and high schools.

Fifteen elementary principals undoubtedly differ on their perceptions of the nature and quality of communications with central office administrators, but there would likely be agreement on the statement that more time is spent communicating than in the past. One reason is that all buildings and offices are linked by telephone and computer networks, making communication easier and faster. Another reason is that the increasing complexities of federal and state rules, regulations, and laws force administrators to come together to learn about and discuss their expanding responsibilities (and liabilities).

On average, elementary principals meet as a group with the assistant superintendent six to eight hours each month—some years once a week; other years, every other week. The agenda is set by the assistant superintendent; however, principals are encouraged to call ahead with their own suggestions for agenda items. In addition, the assistant superintendent meets with principals in smaller groups once each month. The small groups are used to focus on different issues. They also make it easier for the less outspoken principals to express opinions.

One apparent trend is to use e-mail to inform the assistant superintendent about issues and events that require no response on his part. Examples of this kind of notice include: a first-grade teacher is taking her students on a walking field trip to the pet store, or an evening meeting is scheduled with parents to discuss the school homework policy.

Clearly, some building issues are too complicated for e-mail. In these situations, the principal contacts the assistant superintendent by phone (or sends an e-mail message expressing the degree of urgency). If substantial information or data need to be shared, the principal will ordinarily drive to the central office and meet face to face with the appropriate administrator. Most problems are resolved in a single meeting or phone call. Principals can expedite the process by describing the problem succinctly and presenting the assistant superintendent with thoughtful alternatives.

## Evaluation and Supervision of Principals

It seems safe to speculate that most people prefer less supervision to more supervision. Principals are probably no exception. The germane question then ought to be: What does a principal do because she is supervised and evaluated by the superintendent (or assistant superintendent) that is different from what she would do if she were not? A superficial answer is that the good principal does the same thing whether or not she is supervised. This response, however, ignores the possibility that every principal can improve. The better question would be: How can a superintendent make a good principal's performance better and not merely different? Further, how does the superintendent establish criteria that will be used in the evaluation of principals?

Accountability demands from parents, school boards, whole communities, and state legislatures will increasingly influence how principals are evaluated. Establishment of criteria for evaluation of principals that also address popular accountability concerns is a difficult challenge for a superintendent. From a principal's perspective, a reasonable superintendent will involve her principals in establishing these criteria.

To begin with, the superintendent must have reliable information about what each principal does. This reinforces the need for principals to initiate communications with superintendents. It is also incumbent upon the principal's supervisor to observe the principal in his school, preferably interacting with students, parents, and staff. Any evaluation where direct observation is limited to one or two brief walk-throughs of the school building will be correspondingly limited in scope, value, and accuracy.

### Local Trends in Evaluation of Principals

Elementary principals in this district are evaluated on their professional goals, building data, community relations, and teacher conferences. Each principal sets three or four professional goals for himself. The assistant superintendent meets with principals individually (twice a year) to discuss progress on these goals. He also observes each principal in a postobservation conference with a teacher.

In addition, the assistant superintendent evaluates each principal in fifteen different, largely subjective, leadership areas. The final, written evaluation also addresses various building data, including parent involvement at school functions, coverage of curriculum, and standardized test scores. The issues surrounding the latter have the greatest potential for transforming the relationship between central office administrators and principals (and also between principals and teachers!). Increased pressure to raise test scores can cause the relationship to deteriorate at every level, or it will force all educators to communicate frequently and frankly.

Continued local success, in an era of increasing public scrutiny around testing, is contingent upon maintaining three central office achievements: a profound understanding of the complexities of standardized test scores, realistic expectations for improvement, and a willingness and ability to communicate some sense of the first two conditions to the general public—including the media.

## *Conclusion*

Superintendents are expected to kick-start the system. They bring a unique style, a program for change, and a personal vision to each new district. Without the support of the principals, their style will become combative, their programs will remain unimplemented, and their vision will trail away in a vapor of empty rhetoric. The key to that support is communication—of both the listening and the expressing varieties.

For their part, principals need to find a balance between overinforming and overconsulting with the central office on the one hand, and becoming isolated and ignorant on the other. If a principal becomes dependent upon the central office for help to make every decision, both building and central office efficiencies are compromised. If he chooses instead to captain his instructional ship through these troubled waters alone, he had better be very good, or very lucky.

MIKE SCHWINDEN *is principal of the Sunnyside Elementary School in Great Falls, Montana.*

*This author asserts that the most effective relationships between the superintendent and the principal are characterized by trust, loyalty, healthy self-confidence, and mutual support. When these conditions exist, he observes, all stakeholders in the district benefit.*

# 6

# Seven factors affecting the relationship between superintendents and principals

*Joseph A. Shivers*

JUDGING BY MY own experience and by conversations that take place anytime principals get together, one aspect of administrative life that my colleagues and I think about and work at is our relationships with our superintendents. From the principal's perspective, the superintendent is a constituency of one who often ranks in importance with the principal's other three main constituencies: students, staff, and parents.

Superintendent relations exasperate (almost to the point of administrative paralysis) some principals who say things like, "I give up! I never know what my superintendent wants!" Other principals operate like hustlers as they brag about mastering the art of the care and feeding of their superintendents. In general, however, conscientious principals regularly assess their relationships with their superintendents and adjust their performances to become as productive and comfortable in their jobs as possible.

NEW DIRECTIONS FOR SCHOOL LEADERSHIP, NO. 10, WINTER 1998 © JOSSEY-BASS PUBLISHERS

The relationship between principal and superintendent ramifies in two important ways: the general productivity (as measured by student learning) of the school and the district, and the personal productivity and satisfaction of the two administrators. While the actual work of schools—educating students—takes place in class-rooms, interactions between principal and superintendent subtly and directly affect the amount and quality of teacher-student work. In addition, according to Peter Drucker (1974), "Work also has to make a life," and the relationship between the principal and the superintendent determines significantly the quality of life for each.

There is no recipe for establishing and maintaining a positive, pro-ductive relationship between principal and superintendent. There are, however, a variety of identifiable factors that affect the relation-ship. These factors, recognized and manipulated by both parties, can maximize the relationship for productivity and job satisfaction.

## Seven Factors That Impact the Superintendent-Principal Relationship

The following is a list of seven generalizable factors that have had an impact on my relationship with each of the superintendents for whom I have worked. The list is not meant to be exhaustive; it con-tains only the factors that have been most prominent and most familiar in my own experience. I have not included minor factors or factors that I learned about secondhand. In a separate section, I discuss a single, noteworthy factor that is unique to my current job.

### Trust

Trust is the sine qua non of successful relationships. Can I, as princi-pal, trust my superintendent to tell me what I need to know, and can I trust my superintendent to do what he or she says? With mutual trust, the relationship will be as productive as talent and circumstances allow; without trust, wariness and distrust fester and contaminate vir-tually every aspect of the relationship. Distrust is antithetical to opti-mal performance, and if distrust reappears like in-basket items every day, dealing with it eventually wears an administrator down. As a principal, it is in my interest, as well (I hope) as it is in my nature, to be trustworthy. I need to maintain trust with my superintendent not only for personal reasons but also for the sake of my constituencies. When I am representing the interests of my students, my staff, and my parents, I cannot afford to be dismissed as a whiner or doomsayer or someone who minces facts for the sake of professional convenience. Two complements to trust are loyalty and support. Loyalty and support include stating misgivings about a proposal privately and then, once a decision has been made, voicing support (or saying nothing) publicly. Superintendents and principals both talk about loyalty and support. A superintendent said to me after being blindsided publicly by a principal of his, "Joe, there's no loyalty anymore"; likewise, a principal tells me of a former superintendent of his who regularly undermined him in public.

## The General Metaphor of the District

The superintendent is responsible for framing and communicating the purpose of the district. In doing so, he or she identifies explicitly or implicitly the metaphor by which the district will operate. Is education a theater production or a movie performed for the edification and improvement of the students? Then the superintendent and principal function as producer and director, and negotiation over means and ends is continual. Is education a battle or a war against ignorance (or other forces)? Then the two function as general and lieutenant, with the superintendent being a more directive leader. The metaphor itself does not seem to be as important as agreement about the essence of the metaphor and each administrator's role in its public execution.

## The Self-Confidence of Both, But Particularly of the Superintendent

A little swagger is okay; it instills confidence in observers that education is in capable hands. Each administrator must have the confidence, the capacity, and the willingness to deflect credit for successes and to embrace responsibility for failures.

From the principal's point of view, the superintendent needs to give him or her the room and the support to be an effective principal, and that takes confidence on the superintendent's part. The best superintendents are those who place high on Maslow's hierarchy-of-needs list. A self-actualized superintendent is a principal's dream; an insecure, suspicious one is a principal's nightmare. Every innovation, every success that a principal experiences can be regarded as a threat by the insecure superintendent.

Principals also must act with confidence. No superintendent has the time to reassure his or her principals every time they make decisions. My current superintendent is fond of saying that his principals are responsible for everything that takes place from "the curb in"; everything from "the curb out" is his.

### The Competence (or Perceived Competence) of Each, Which in Turn Is Tied to Self-Confidence

As principal, I want to know what the strengths and weaknesses of my superintendent are. For example, if I want the superintendent to give a pep talk to my faculty or if my students would benefit from a motivational speech before they begin standardized testing, I need to know if public speaking is a strength of his or hers. If the competencies of the two are complementary, service to students, staff, and parents is improved. When one can call on the expertise of the other with confidence, both become sharper in their jobs.

### The Age and Aspirations of Each

The tenure of educational administrators is typically not long; in Ohio some refer to superintendents and principals as the world's highest paid migrant workers. The age and aspirations of both parties affect the length of their relationship and the depth of their relationship. If either senses, for example, that the other will not be around long because of impending retirement or because of aspirations to move on to something more attractive, the relationship changes. If there is a major disagreement between the two, one may simply hunker down and wait out the other.

## The Size of the District

In smaller districts the superintendent has more time to spend with each principal, and principals have more opportunities to see their superintendents. The superintendent as symbol can accomplish a great deal, including increasing a principal's stock, by visiting schools.

A second advantage that small districts hold for principal-superintendent relations is that in such districts principals often have systemwide duties, such as curriculum director or testing coordinator, in addition to their building-level responsibilities. Although the principal is still answerable to the superintendent, the two become ad hoc colleagues; they work in tandem, cooperating on issues that affect students and staff throughout the system.

In large districts, fact-to-face, informal encounters are usually less common; consequently, regularly scheduled, formal meetings are more important to the nurture of principal-superintendent relations.

In any district, the quality and quantity of interactions bear directly on the relationship; familiarity breeds familiarity. (A third party, the superintendent's secretary, can broker the superintendent-principal relationship if he or she tenaciously guards the boss's time and the information that comes in and goes out of the central office. The attentive principal must work to include the secretary in his or her approach to superintendent relations.)

## Gender, Ethnicity, Race, Class, Religion

I have not experienced the potentially polarizing effects of these factors because I have always been of the same gender, race, and class as my superintendent and have been similar in ethnicity and religion. I have never had a female superintendent or a superintendent of color. In my jobs so far, this factor has been important because of the impact it has not had. Female colleagues of mine, however, who work with male superintendents tell me that a variety of issues regularly arise because of the gender difference.

---

## A Special Factor

The seven factors previously listed are the ones that have affected most saliently and most consistently the relationships I have had with my first five superintendents. With my sixth superintendent, however, comes a special factor: close friendship. My current superintendent and I are friends—close friends. We are not just two people who were first-year teachers together and gradually began to pal around, or two guys who had coached against one another for years and developed a friendship over time. Rather we became friends so long ago that neither of us remembers exactly when our friendship began. We went to kindergarten, elementary school, and junior high and high school together. We were in Boy Scouts together, lived on the same street five houses from one another, attended the same church, and double-dated in high school. Each of us served as best man in the other's wedding. We share the same first name. Superimpose a long-standing friendship over the seven factors listed above—or over any set of factors—and the friendship subsumes them all. When the superintendent and principal are lifelong friends, their friendship becomes the most important factor to be considered in their professional relationship.

Imagine a relationship between yourself and your superintendent in which you know all the nuances of the affiliation going in. Imagine a job in which, from the day you are hired, there is never any thought but that the superintendent has your interests at heart. Starting in a new district and acquainting yourself with rules and procedures—however extensive—is easier than learning and adjusting to the personality and philosophy of the stranger who happens to be your boss.

Issues that colleagues say they worry about are not issues in my job. I never think about underlying motives in anything Joe says or does that involves me or my students or my staff. I never worry about not getting his best efforts. On the other hand, I do things for Joe that I might rationalize not doing for others. There are times when logistics or personal comfort argue that I not volunteer for some duty or responsibility or that I not take up a suggestion that means adding to or changing what I already do. When Joe asks me to do something that I possibly can do, and I have a choice, I say "Yes." With Joe I do not distinguish between personal and professional requests.

What is more, my motivation to exploit my talents and shore up my weaknesses in the pursuit of excellence seems to be greater working with Joe. Do not misunderstand me. Wherever I have worked, I have taken pride in using all of my abilities and giving my best efforts on behalf of the people who have employed me to oversee the education of their children. I am very competitive; I am unafraid of long hours; I am motivated to do well as a principal; and—judging by common, public standards and by my own personal standards—I have had a successful career as an educator. Working for Joe, however, brings out something more in me. He, too, is clever and creative and relentless in the pursuit of educational excellence. He, too, is very competitive. (In fact, competition—as teammates and as rivals—has always been part of our friendship.) His expectations for educators working for him are high. His expectations for himself, however, are higher and clearer than any I have ever known, outside of my own. My current superintendent and I have a comfortable, low-maintenance professional relationship because it fits within the generous boundaries of our personal friendship; most issues that could affect our relationship today were resolved long ago.

Our friendship can become a professional encumbrance in two circumstances: when people perceive that Joe favors me in an administrative decision, and when I hear criticism of Joe.

As far as Joe favoring me and my school is concerned, our friendship permits clear and generous bounds for him to do just the opposite. I think that I make it easy for Joe to recognize others first when he is allocating the district's tangible resources as well as his administrative time and attention. Public criticism of Joe is another matter. Whenever I hear or read something unflattering about him, I tend to react emotionally before responding rationally. I have always refrained from criticizing my staff and my boss publicly. Taking cheap shots at people I work with has always seemed cowardly and unproductive, if not counterproductive. In the past, however, if I overheard something negative about my superintendent, I could make a reasoned decision to keep quiet. Now, however, I am able to let gratuitous criticism pass only with much effort.

Let me be clear. I do not agree with Joe on every issue: our educational philosophies diverge from time to time. Furthermore, I let him know when I disagree with him, and he does the same with me. But agreeing to disagree is more comfortable and more instructive when it occurs between friends. The momentum of forty-five years of friendship overcomes a great many obstacles.

## Conclusion

I am not sure what useful educational leadership model could be built on an experience as exclusive as a close friendship. (Although, many of the professional advantages that stem from friendship are ones that any two administrators could work toward.) I do know that even if all seven factors align, the resulting relationship can be synergistic or it can be sterile. What seems to make the difference is how much each likes the other.

In education, at least in a smaller district, so much depends on the principal-superintendent relationship. In ten years as a principal I have worked with six superintendents, and I have learned about professional and personal relationships from all of them. In each case, both my superintendent and I have been better professionals when our relationship has been attended to thoughtfully and carefully. Understanding the factors that affect relationships makes it easier, in turn, for pairs of administrators to develop and maintain their relationships to their mutual benefit and to the benefit of their students, staff, and community.

*Reference*

Drucker, P. *Management: Tasks, Responsibilities, Practices.* New York: Harper-Collins, 1974.

JOSEPH A. SHIVERS *is principal of Columbiana High School in Columbiana, Ohio.*

*In recognition of the unique relationship enjoyed by this superintendent with the principal author of the previous chapter, the first half of this chapter is a commentary on the principal's framework for thinking about the relationship. Factors such as perceived professional competence and career cycles are explored. The second half of the chapter offers a personal account of their lifelong friendship and its impact on their work as administrators in the same school district.*

# 7

# Friends and colleagues: A response to the factors suggested by Joseph A. Shivers affecting the relationship between a superintendent and a principal

*Joe Rottenborn*

REGARDING THE FACTORS Joseph A. Shivers lists that affect the relationship between these two positions in educational administration, trust certainly does seem to be of prime importance. Of course, trust goes both ways: the superintendent's trust of the principal and vice versa. For the superintendent to trust the principal, he or she must believe a number of things about the principal. Superintendents must feel that principals will support them, not try to undermine

NEW DIRECTIONS FOR SCHOOL LEADERSHIP, NO. 10, WINTER 1998 © JOSSEY-BASS PUBLISHERS

their authority, undercut them, or "make them look bad." If the superintendent cannot feel this way, a productive relationship will likely be impossible. From their perspective, principals must be convinced that the superintendent will be candid with them, will stand behind them, and, simply, will respect them as the building leader. Without this conviction, the principal is not likely to desire to develop a relationship with his or her superintendent.

From the superintendent's perspective, much of this trust stems from his or her evaluation of the principal's competence, another factor affecting their relationship. For the superintendent knows that, if the principal is competent, ultimately, the superintendent will be more likely to be judged as successful than if the principal is not competent.

As for the second factor on Shivers's list, the general metaphor by which the district operates, this is typically, though not always, determined by the superintendent. Regardless of what the metaphor is, however, the extent to which a principal embraces this metaphor and acts accordingly will likely influence his or her relationship with the superintendent. Simply put, a superintendent wants key players in the district—particularly, building principals and other members of the management team—"on the same page." Superintendents value highly those principals who believe in the district's vision and work to carry it out. The esteem of the superintendent for such a principal helps a relationship to develop between them.

The third factor specified, the self-confidence of both the superintendent and the principal, also derives from a number of variables, including how long each has served in his or her position, the success each has had (in the current and previous assignments), and a host of other variables, some professional, others, perhaps, more personal. It might be posited, however, that the closer the relationship a superintendent and principal have, the more likely both will be able to feel self-confident, since each benefits from the support the other provides.

Competence, real or perceived, is critical to a relationship between a superintendent and a principal, since both, to a degree, put their career's success into the hands of the other. How well each is judged will be related to how effectively the other performs in his or her position. Experience, graduate training, and intelligence may affect the assessment of how competent a superintendent and principal view each other to be. But, in the end, the most important variable may simply be how good each perceives the other to be in doing his or her job. A superintendent who doubts the competence of a particular principal will likely have more difficulty establishing a relationship with that administrator than if he or she views the principal as competent. The reverse is probably also the case.

As for the age and aspirations of both, it seems typical for a superintendent to give older or experienced principals "the benefit of the doubt" in administering their buildings, at least initially or until this stance proves unwise. With younger, less-experienced principals, a superintendent would seem more likely to advise them directly or, indeed, even act as their mentor. Regarding the aspirations of each, superintendents who desire to move to larger or more desirable districts, based on a successful performance in their current position, might try to develop relationships with principals to enhance their chances of current success, and thereby facilitate their desired career move. Superintendents planning to remain in a particular district may be less concerned with current success from their principals, knowing that, if principals fail, the principals, not the superintendent, will likely face the most immediate—and serious—consequences. As far as the aspirations of principals are concerned, superintendents who are trusting and self-confident, and who perceive themselves to be competent will not probably feel threatened by principals who aspire to be superintendents. Indeed, such a superintendent will often advise and aid the principal in attaining this goal. On the other hand, superintendents who are not trusting, self-confident, or competent may fear principals who desire to be superintendents, which can affect negatively the development of a relationship between these two administrators.

The size of a district can affect the relationship between a superintendent and a principal if it influences the number and quality of interactions, face to face or by telephone, the two administrators engage in. In large districts where a superintendent and principal may not communicate on a daily or even a weekly basis, there would seem to be less opportunity for a relationship between the two to develop than in a smaller district, in which a superintendent and principal interact more frequently, often on a daily basis.

The final factor, gender/ethnicity/race/class, is also important to consider, though the size and nature of the district might determine how crucial this factor is in a particular situation. In smaller, rural districts, gender might exert more influence than, say, ethnicity or race; while in larger, urban districts, all facets of this final factor would, perhaps, be more operative.

---

## Comments on Factors Affecting the Relationship Between Superintendent and Principal: A Personal Case Study

I first met Joe Shivers, a principal in the small (total student enrollment: 1,050) Ohio district in which I have served as superintendent for the last four years, on our first day of kindergarten. It was at the Buckeye Elementary School in the small town of Salem, Ohio. During that first year of our formal schooling, we became good friends. We were classmates through eight years at St. Paul School in Salem, sharing many experiences, both in the classroom and in afterschool activities like baseball, basketball, and Cub Scouts/Boy Scouts. In high school, Joe moved to the same street where I had always lived; we often walked together, then rode, to Salem High School, where we continued having similar experiences in classrooms, athletics, and social activities. Following graduation, we maintained our friendship, keeping in contact throughout college and working in the same factory during the summers. Ultimately, he became my closest friend, serving as best man at my wedding, while I served as best man at his.

As for mutual educational endeavors, I served as a pilot interviewee during his dissertation research; he conducted the interviewing for my doctoral study. Professionally, we both became public school administrators, though working in different Ohio districts until the summer of 1997, when I recommended his hiring as our district's middle school principal.

Our long and close friendship, which has now developed into a professional relationship between superintendent and principal, is, to be sure, uncommon. As such, however, it offers a particular perspective not often seen on the factors affecting the relationship between a superintendent and a principal.

Regarding the factor of trust between this superintendent and principal, that is a given—developed over forty-five years of association. I know he would never do anything to hurt me and he knows the same of me. We are, unquestionably, loyal to each other. I support him and vice versa; we provide both private and public compliments as well as deflect criticism directed toward each other. As a result of this firm trust, we are free to be more open, candid, and, yes, vulnerable with each other in a way a superintendent and principal typically might not be. Consequently, we can be "on the same page," working cooperatively together for the best interests of the children in our district.

Insofar as the general metaphor our district employs, it may change from time to time. Sometimes, it seems, we are engaged in a theater or movie production, while, at other times, we do seem to be involved in a battle or, occasionally, a war. On most days, however, we are involved in what seems like a game to be won. But, on all days, the mutual competitiveness of both superintendent and principal enhances our relationship. Frankly, neither of us likes to lose, and therefore we do what is required to perform our jobs well. The mutual trait of competitiveness we share, rather than the district's particular metaphor, has had a bonding effect on our relationship.

As for the self-confidence of this superintendent and principal, it has been acquired in sufficient measure through lives and careers involving the accomplishing of both personal and professional goals. Personally, both of us are blessed to have long, stable, and happy marriages to supportive women from our same hometown; each family has two healthy, bright children. Professionally, the superintendent has derived self-confidence from a productive career in both teaching and administration, having achieved a capstone position for most in K–12 education, and recently, completing the terminal doctoral degree. The principal earned his doctorate at an Ivy League university, has served successfully as a school administrator for the last decade, and was chosen to be president of the Ohio Middle School Association. Thus, both possess self-confidence and have no need to try to impress—or, ever, intimidate—the other. As a result, their relationship, enhanced by mutual respect, flourishes.

The competence the superintendent recognizes in this principal has been observed over almost a lifetime of common experiences. From elementary school to secondary grades, through college and graduate school, the superintendent has witnessed the intelligence of this principal. In the superintendent's view, the principal is the most well-educated person he knows. Over the past school year, the superintendent has heard and watched the principal carrying out his administrative duties, since their offices are only twenty-five feet apart in the same building. From the perspective of these multiple vantage points, the superintendent views this principal as extremely competent, well qualified to handle all matters pertaining to his building, "from the curb in," which is the district's expectation of its principals.

Regarding the age and aspirations of both the superintendent and principal, both are the same age, fifty years old. Furthermore, each is happy in his current position, enjoying the challenges—and opportunities—of his job. Both enjoy the chance to work with each other on a daily basis, an experience that is deepening their personal and professional relationships.

Given the small size of the district in which the superintendent and principal work, their contacts with each other are frequent and informal. Typically, they talk many times daily, face to face and by phone, usually without bothering to schedule appointments. In short, they communicate like they have been doing it their whole lives—because they have been. On a foundation of such frequent communication, relationships can grow. And this one has.

Finally, the gender/ethnicity/race/class factor is another bonding factor between this superintendent and principal, since both are white males who come from the same small-town middle class. Furthermore, they share the Catholic religion, Democratic politics, and affection for sports teams (the Cleveland Indians, the Cleveland Browns, and as a result of both having attended college in Boston, the Celtics). They are probably as similar in background as a superintendent and principal could be.

In sum, then, this superintendent and principal not only know each other and respect each other, but, perhaps more important, like each other. As a result, they have a relationship that empowers both, enabling each to perform to his maximum capability.

JOE ROTTENBORN *is superintendent of schools for the Columbiana Exempted Village Schools in Columbiana, Ohio.*

*As the only principal member on the National Commission on Teaching and America's Future, the author describes its conclusions and how the relationship between principals and superintendents is central to the commission's vision. This complex relationship is characterized as creative and as such, the author argues, in need of hyphenated roles that allow flexibility beyond the official organizational structure. Just as the teacher can be a teacher-mentor, teacher-researcher, and teacher-leader, so too should the principals and superintendents strive to be cast in roles that allow them maximum fluidity and relational leadership.*

# 8

# Crossing boundaries: Principals and superintendents assume multiple roles and collaborate in a climate of creative tension

*Lynn F. Stuart*

OVER TWO YEARS AGO the National Commission on Teaching and America's Future published findings that were based at once on research and common sense. The National Commission determined that "What Matters Most" (1996) in achieving a

NEW DIRECTIONS FOR SCHOOL LEADERSHIP, NO. 10, WINTER 1998 © JOSSEY-BASS PUBLISHERS

quality education is ensuring a competent, caring, and qualified teacher for every student in America—a tall order in an era of muddled, often piecemeal solutions to America's reform of education. However, the National Commission's work offered a comprehensive set of recommendations which, for the first time in the recent decades of reform, offered an integrated, interconnected picture of possibility for dramatically improving our children's education.

The National Commission raised the simple but troubling question of what everyone associated with education does to support those on the front lines. It identified the needs to improve teacher recruitment, preparation, induction, professional development and recognition across a teacher's career, and, more important, the organization of schools to support teacher learning and student success. Nestled in the report is the belief that these recommendations rely heavily on the school principal and school district leaders to create the conditions in schools where competent teaching thrives. The National Commission focused on the broad landscape of what it takes to create a teaching force that is competent. It is against this backdrop that I want to discuss the essential roles of the principal and the superintendent in supporting teacher quality in every school.

## The "Pendulum Dilemma"

Another important aspect of the educational landscape provides a glimpse of the context in which we struggle to improve learning and teaching. Teachers and administrators are confronted daily with what I call the "pendulum dilemma." The "pendulum dilemma" presents the false dichotomy of what appear to be contradictory forces that swing back and forth from truth to demon. It is easy to name these forces: human development and exploration versus rigor and accountability, community learning versus individual learning, writing versus spelling, concepts versus computation in mathematics, portfolios versus testing, school versus district, district versus state, change versus stability, and so on. Teachers, families, and the public are held hostage by the current moment's swing of the pendulum. Many teachers simply ignore the current swing, remaining entrenched wherever they are, waiting for the next swing to offer old mandates . . . again. New teachers are confused by the contradictions of teacher preparation and practice, and with the push-pull of district policies and school-based initiatives. Both ends of the pendulum swing have merit; it is simply that each by itself neglects the complexity of human learning and teaching. Instead of asking the either/or question, we might better ask, "How do we integrate the ideas reflected across a continuum in a balanced way?"

The only way we can emerge from the pendulum dilemma and create the conditions of teaching envisioned by the National Commission is to rediscover the notions of continuum and balance. However, the path we must take is not one of a middle road but rather a path that both examines the known and leads us into new territory. It is a path that requires new definitions of leadership. A redefinition of leadership as seen in the roles and the relationships of principals and superintendents and their relationships to teachers can help to clarify and move the profession to a new place.

## *Redefining Leadership*

We have been mired in a hierarchy defined by power *over* rather than power *with* colleagues on different rungs of the hierarchical ladder. Not that hierarchy is to be condemned—that would once again ignore the complexity of the organizational continuum. However, linear, vertical relationships with their fixed borders of responsibility and authority impede the possibility of truly creative, collaborative work. The power of leadership is relational, that is, achieved in relationship to human connection, to collaboration, rather than merely to authority. Fear of authority causes individuals and organizations to stagnate. Fear undermines the creative powers of risk-taking and redefining roles. It diminishes energy or forces it to go underground. Authority without relationship is narrow and short-sighted. At a time when we dearly need leadership, some districts have created a climate in which single measures of student achievement are the basis for hiring and retaining principals, teachers, or superintendents. Such a narrow view of accountability has deleterious effects, including teaching to the test, possible manipulation of test scores, and a climate of playing it safe. Fear in the classroom has a similar effect. Doors close, teachers become dogmatic and rule-driven. Creativity and teamwork fade. Isolation creates a buffer zone but stifles collaborative growth. That is why the ends of the continuum represented on the one hand by the principal/manager under unilateral district control and on the other hand by the charter school movement in which secession eliminates the "repressive" bureaucracy are both ill-conceived. To free ourselves from the pendulum dilemma, we must reinvent leadership, from the ground up and from the top down.

## Leading from the Front and from Behind

When I was hired as a principal, it was clear to me that the school community wanted a principal who could lead both from the front and from behind. I have often thought about that concept and the power that this dual nature of leadership engenders. Leading from the front at the district or school level creates a vision and coherence that can and must be shared. It establishes authority and accountability. It establishes the role of guide, facilitator, and change leader when opportunities and needs for change arise. Leading from behind creates confidence in the leader's responsibility to know his or her community well. Sensitive observation has always been a key to competent teaching. It is the chief vehicle for knowing learners well. Likewise, listening and observing closely help a principal to know the needs of the community and draw on the leadership and strengths of others.

Leading from behind is a key to establishing the respect of the community with which one works. It legitimizes authority in the form of collaborative leadership. Accomplishment rests with the community as well as with the leader when principals lead from behind. A principal who can stand courageously in front and at the same time develop the confidence and shared leadership of his or her community is one who can weather the ambiguities, roadblocks, and failures that undermine efforts to strengthen teaching. Superintendents often lead from the front. Can they, too, learn the importance of leading from behind?

## Multiple Roles

Leading from behind also invites teacher leadership and the power of what I call "hyphenated roles" that value teaching while nurturing leadership. Such roles for teachers might be seen as teacher-researcher, teacher-mentor, teacher-curriculum leader, teacher-administrator, and the like. These hyphenated roles imply that professional growth and contribution need not require leaving the classroom and, at the same time, that teacher leadership flourishes outside the classroom as well. Perhaps it is time to think about hyphenated roles for principals, curriculum administrators, and superintendents too. The origin of the principalship came from the notion of "principal teacher," implying that once the principal was indeed close to the classroom and to the lives of teachers and students. In modern times, the superintendent's role has been more clearly defined as a policy role, connected to the school committee and the setting of direction for an entire district. Effective leadership for a teacher, curriculum leader, principal, or superintendent depends on the capacity of the school district to support and strengthen professional relationships in all the nuances of multiple roles. This means that as the teacher's base for leadership starts and then expands from the classroom, the principal's and superintendent's base for leadership starts from a broader place and then spirals back to the classrooms where the essence of formal education resides.

If the power of collaboration is at the heart of leadership, let's look now at the ways in which the roles of superintendent and principal connect and, indeed, sometimes collide. Differences of perspective are derived from the nature of the two roles. A principal's mandate is to serve the school. However, serving the school does not mean failing to be an active participant in working on the needs and issues of the district. A superintendent's goal is to lead the district, which consists of multiple schools at different levels. But that does not mean that policy can be developed independent of the complexity of the different needs of the various schools. The superintendent and his or her team face the dilemma of every parent: paying attention to the individual and being fair to all members of the family while developing policies that serve all students and teachers well. If respect, fairness, and communication are at the heart of a healthy family, then they are also at the heart of a healthy organization.

Reinventing the organization of schools and districts is the mutual task of today's leaders. If the central office should no longer be the sole power broker in the district and if schools should not be islands of excellence, mediocrity, or dysfunction, then new structures and relationships must be invented to create a district that has clear, negotiated standards and working mechanisms. For the whole and its parts to be in a mutually renewing relationship, policies that guide the work must provide consistent processes for accomplishing goals. The tension between process and product must be addressed. In the rush "to get the job done," to vastly improve schools, there is also the danger of expedience. A result without a process that has been understood and participatory is often short-lived. Paying attention to process, while often messy and time-consuming, generates the clarity of purpose, broad support, and community investment to sustain growth and change. Reducing bureaucratic roadblocks and increasing communication, creating an openness to possibility while at the same time maintaining predictability, creating rituals and stories to weave into the life of the organization—these are tasks that are necessary if we are to recharge and renew organizational health.

## Institutionalizing Creative Tension

What structures can be put into place to institutionalize a creative tension in the relationship between the superintendent and the principal? Creative tension is a central facet of strong relationships. Creative tension implies respect for different visions and taking steps to accomplish them. It implies stability and change—a negotiation of viewpoints, a moving forward with purpose in negotiation. Creative tension in this discussion focuses on relationships and is thus distinguished from the definition of creative tension in the context of vision and current reality that is used by Peter Senge and referenced in the chapter contributed by Superintendent D'Alessandro.

Creative tension should be in place in the school setting, with the principal and teachers jointly exploring ways to strengthen teaching and learning. Our school uses its staff, cluster, and grade-level team meetings as the principal vehicles for communication. An annual school summer workshop and alternative professional time (which is provided weekly or biweekly during the school day for each staff member for about fifteen weeks annually) also serve as venues for our discussion and formulation of school initiatives and policies on curriculum, assessment, and their implications for learning. We have a protocol for analyzing student work that is collected in portfolios and maintained across the grades in the school archive. Our assessments of student learning (via portfolios, performance tasks, and standardized tests) are reviewed to discover all the ways a student demonstrates what she or he knows and is able to do. We have developed ways to share our own professional development initiatives with each other. Last year we sponsored a teacher who applied to the National Board for Professional Teaching Standards for advanced certification, and she in turn shared the rigorous application process with us. School-based courses to investigate questions about race, class, and culture, or to study troubled and troubling children, have further grounded us in our own learning and development. We publish annual and ongoing descriptions of the planned and implemented curriculum of the school. And we work with families to provide forums to share what we know about our students as families share what they know about their children. The journey is not always smooth, but the commitment of the faculty to work together and with families to build the school culture, learning environment, and strong expectations for all children is evident. And there is a sense, in the wise words of one of our teachers, that "we disagree well with each other."

Creative tension also tempers and guides the relationship of the principal and the superintendent. It is essential to have multiple forums for open and honest communication. We suffer the problem of too many meetings, but not enough communication. In fact, I believe that probably more meetings rather than fewer meetings are necessary, with some focused on a topic, some study sessions, some sharing/informational sessions, some brainstorming sessions. In our medium-sized urban district, we should be able to meet occasionally as one unit. Larger districts clearly need to create communication groups that are manageable in size with some large-scale meetings where all share the same information.

## Communication

We must also reach out to the larger community. New partnerships with health, human service, law enforcement, business, and civic organizations must be created at the district level with participation of principals and teachers. And not to be forgotten in the communication process is the dramatic need to strengthen the relationships between schools and colleges of education. The disconnect between teacher education and schools cannot be justified, especially in an era when we will be hiring two million new teachers nationwide.

Communication must also take place in more intimate surroundings—at the school or in small groups based on shared needs or interests. Just as I must be accessible to my school community and be a good observer and listener, I expect that the superintendent needs to play that role with me and my school. It is not enough for any leader to say he or she supports his or her constituents; active involvement must demonstrate that commitment.

Goal setting on the part of the principal and supervision by the superintendent are an integral part of the communication process, generating a creative, critical review of work that is ongoing, affirmative, and also rich in suggestion for new ways of thinking and acting. Supervision is always an important aspect of leadership. Strong leaders use supervision as an opportunity for collaboration—a chance to observe, listen, debate, probe, and extend the boundaries of knowledge for the supervisor and the supervisee. Problems arise chiefly when supervision is aborted and becomes a one-time evaluation outside the context of a relationship of working together over time.

As principals and superintendents engage in the work of creating multiple roles, creative tension is visible in many arenas. The superintendent participates in portfolio reviews of student work. The principal participates in the design of districtwide accountability structures and data systems for monitoring student achievement. Principals' voices are heard in the hiring and professional development activities of their faculties. The superintendent holds principals accountable for personnel leadership and also works to reduce bureaucratic stumbling blocks to timely and efficient hiring. Districtwide initiatives for new, early career teachers, midcareer teachers, and teacher-leaders are guided by the superintendent's leadership in providing a coherent vision for professional development. One of the most vital overlapping roles both principal and superintendent play is mentoring. Strong leaders are mentors for the rising generation of leaders. This is a powerful cycle of growth in which principals are mentors for teachers and superintendents are mentors for principals.

## Dangers of Breakdown in Creative Tension

The potential dangers of a breakdown in creative tension in the relationship between principal and superintendent are nowhere more apparent than in the issues of accountability for student achievement. We live in a high-stakes climate. Accountability is important, and the measures of accountability need to be as varied as the many definitions of competence. A principal is likely to understand competence across many disciplines. A principal knows the students: they are human beings who demonstrate competence in many ways. Documentation of these many ways of demonstrating what students can and cannot do is the key to validating and improving competence for students and teachers alike. A principal also knows that the school and central office must redirect resources to help teachers improve individual student achievement. A superintendent must be able to check on the learning of the many. Is the district performing up to its stated goals? Are all students reaching standards and their highest potential? Is there equality of opportunity? If not, how can the school and the district provide new supports and new forms of teaching to improve performance? Principals and superintendents can play it safe and focus all their efforts on teaching to the current testing system. But in a profession that transcends the pendulum dilemma, principals and superintendents should be able to build new bridges to multiple forms of assessment, from in-depth, independent portfolio reviews at key grade levels to performance assessments to snapshot tests of all students at certain grades. Genuine accountability also encompasses a broad range of school and district practices as they relate to standards for teaching, standards for schools, and standards for the system. As Darling-Hammond notes, "A genuinely accountable system recognizes that school problems can be caused as much by district and state policies such as unequal funding, hiring and assignment of unqualified personnel, and counterproductive curriculum policies as they are by conditions within the school" (1997, p. 248). Indeed, shared accountability is essential for student success.

## *Walking in Each Other's Shoes*

Building a culture in which creative tension flourishes both within the school and within the district is a clear sign of a robust organization. It is a place where both affirmation and disagreement abound as inquiry and reflection guide the participants in their work. Such a culture creates an environment of learning. That is our mission for students; it must be no less the mission for all who work with and support students.

In front and behind, principals and superintendents are inextricably connected. Their relationship to each other and to teachers in the school and the district holds the possibility for new models of leadership that support competent, caring, qualified teachers in every classroom.

All the students in our school learn songs that carry the powerful message of collaboration and community. One of them begins and echoes throughout, "I'm gonna walk, walk, walk, a mile in your shoes. . . ." Another of our favorite school songs (Wyatt, 1994) reminds us in Spanish that "Somos el barco, somos el mar; yo navego en ti, tu navegas en mi" (We are the boat, we are the sea, I sail in you, you sail in me). We cannot understand our various roles and responsibilities without crossing the boundaries of our own images of our individual roles into the land of the other. This simple concept is so often forgotten in organizational life, yet it is a key to a healthy organization. Schools thrive in a climate of creative tension where teachers, principals, and superintendents search for continuity and balance while at the same time pushing beyond the boundaries of the known.

## References

Darling-Hammond, L. *The Right to Learn: A Blueprint for Creating Schools That Work*. San Francisco: Jossey-Bass, 1997.

National Commission on Teaching and America's Future. *What Matters Most: Teaching and America's Future*. New York: National Commission on Teaching and America's Future, 1996.

Nigro, J. "Walk a Mile." Ithaca, N.Y.: Lovable Creature Music, 1994.

Wyatt, L. "Somos el Barco." In *Cambridgeport School's Greatest Hits, 1990–1994*. Cambridge, Mass.: Friends of the Cambridgeport School, 1994.

LYNN F. STUART *is principal of the Cambridgeport School in Cambridge, Massachusetts.*

*This chapter describes how the relationship between the superintendent and the principal is built upon the trust that comes from mutual respect, frequent communication, and shared identification as teachers. The author articulates three factors that determine the type of relationship the dyad will have: multiplicity of roles, context of the district, and specific qualities that promote a solid partnership.*

# 9

# Taking turns at teaching and learning: The superintendent-principal partnership

*Bobbie D'Alessandro*

INSTRUCTIONAL LEADERS are critical to the achievement of the educational goals and mission set forth in a school district. Seemingly, the two most important instructional leaders are the principal at the building level and the superintendent at the district level. One could argue that the relationship between these two individuals would have to be strong when there is open communication, mutual trust and respect, and clear expectations of each individual. Furthermore, given the multitude of complex issues confronting educators on a daily basis, as well as the various roles that each will play at some point in the relationship (for example, mentor/mentee, supervisor/supervisee), it is imperative that this relationship go

NEW DIRECTIONS FOR SCHOOL LEADERSHIP, NO. 10, WINTER 1998 © JOSSEY-BASS PUBLISHERS

beyond collegiality to one that challenges and invigorates both individuals.

The relationship between a superintendent and a principal has not been studied to any great extent. Much of the literature on this relationship is anecdotal. However, the characteristics of each leader, with regards to the other, are articulated in numerous articles and books (see Bolman and Deal, 1997; Hayden, 1990; Johnson, 1996). The lack of specific attention to this precious relationship could be problematic in the face of educational reform. As site-based management and accountability become laypeople's terms, educational leadership must be coordinated to deliver the best services to its clientele. This chapter addresses the three factors that I feel define the relationship between a superintendent and a principal working toward coordination of service delivery. These are (1) multiplicity in roles, (2) context of the district, and (3) specific qualities that promote (or not) a solidly built relationship.

## Duplicitous Relationships

Within dyads, each member plays a primary role and at any given point may also take on secondary roles depending on the circumstances. Such is the case in the superintendent-principal dyad. For example, a superintendent may act as a mentor, a friend, a supervisor, and an evaluator to a new or experienced principal depending on the task or issue at hand. What must be defined, either formally or informally, is the role being enacted at that specific time. In the case of an evaluation, the superintendent must be prepared to give positive feedback as well as suggestions for improvement; thus the superintendent would be acting appropriately as an evaluator. During an evaluation, the principal is given feedback on the success of his or her school. It is important that friendship not cloud the evaluation. When acting as a mentor, the superintendent must remain patient and receptive to new ideas as the principal learns and develops into a strong educational leader. In this case, though the principal is still accountable to the superintendent, there may be greater room for mistakes than in a high-stakes evaluation. Encouraging risk-taking is important; therefore a safety net must be built in to ensure learning whether or not the project is ultimately successful. The two leaders must continually review and clarify their roles in the relationship.

Regularly scheduled formal and informal meetings allow the superintendent and the principal to get to know each other in a personal and professional manner; the building of trust occurs in one-on-one meetings. Understanding each other's educational philosophies and approaches to problem solving nurtures a new and expanded relationship, one that can, over time, benefit both people. Taking turns being teacher and learner naturally occurs when the superintendent and the principal share a commitment to their relationship.

Given that the superintendent formally supervises the principal, it is the superintendent's responsibility to clearly convey his or her intentions to the principal. As Hayden (1990) asserts, no matter what role the superintendent takes on at a particular time, "principals could not successfully assume or enact their role unless the role of the district superintendent is understood, the expectations the superintendent held for them as principals are known, and how the roles fit into a total organizational context" (p. 2).

*Context*

School districts are difficult and demanding places in which to work. Educational leaders are engaged in constant negotiations with various constituents to prove their efficacy in the field. The state makes demands on superintendents to raise test scores; parents hold principals responsible for the well-being of their children during the school day; the media reports the failures of education more consistently than they report the successes. Whether the district is in turmoil or in the midst of positive change, the issues that arise out of these situations can easily strain the relationship between the superintendent and the principal. Freedom for individuals to "tell it like it is" is imperative for the relationship to grow and develop positively.

Peter Senge, in his work "The Leader's New Work: Building Learning Organizations" (1990), presents a discussion about creative tension, which he calls the "integrating principle." According to Senge,

Leadership in a learning organization starts with the principle of creative tension . . . [which] comes from seeing clearly where we want to be, our "vision," and telling the truth about where we are, our "current reality." Creative tension can be resolved in two basic ways: by raising current reality toward the vision, or by lowering the vision toward the current reality. Individuals, groups and organizations who learn how to work with creative tension learn how to use the energy it generates to move reality more reliably toward their visions. . . . [W]ithout vision there is no creative tension. . . . [C]reative tension cannot be generated from current reality alone. All the analysis in the world will never generate a vision. But creative tension cannot be generated from vision alone: it demands an accurate picture of current reality as well. Vision without an understanding of current reality will more likely foster cynicism than creativity. The principle of creative tension teaches that an accurate picture of current reality is just as important as a compelling picture of a desired future. . . . With creative tension, the energy for change comes from the vision, from what we want to create, juxtaposed with current reality. With creative tension, the motivation is intrinsic. This distinction mirrors the distinction between adaptive and generative learning [p. 9 ].

As stated above, schools are increasingly being challenged and are often forced to accept educational reform initiatives regardless of how they feel about them. Sometimes what the superintendent believes would be best suited for a particular school is not the reform the principal, teachers, or parents in that school accept. A battle of wills ensues: each wants to reform the educational program, but each differs on how it should be done. The principal and the superintendent should regularly discuss the vision for the school system and align the school's work with systemwide goals. Communication with all stakeholders about current reality and enlisting their help to accomplish the goals are essential. Clearly, broad-based involvement can ease tension and provide an excellent venue for participation in the process that will result in positive future commitments.

Another contextual factor in the building of the superintendent-principal relationship is each individual's history with other superintendents and principals. The average length of tenure for an urban superintendent is 2.5 years (Cuban, 1998). Feasibly, principals could see as many as seven or eight superintendents during their tenures, each of whom has his or her own leadership style. Thus, principals may grow very weary of new superintendents, particularly if they had a strained relationship with another superintendent. Concurrently, superintendents may have left a district because of a disagreement with a principals' union or a particular principal's style. Should a superintendent encounter a principal similar to one with whom he or she had conflict in the past, he or she may well begin a new relationship with beliefs that the current one will be as unproductive as the previous one. In either case, superintendents and principals must negotiate with each other about the confines and expectations of the relationship. Honesty with one another is an essential element in an effective superintendent-principal relationship.

Finally, there are compounding factors that must be considered in any professional relationship. These include the gender, race, ethnicity, and experiential base of each of the individuals. Superintendents and principals are not immune to the effects of these personal characteristics as they manifest themselves in a professional relationship. Again, both the superintendent and the principal must acknowledge and deal with their own issues arising from these factors. Conflict should be openly discussed and agreements made on how to strengthen future work.

## Qualities of the Relationship

In many professional relationships, supervisors are in daily, direct contact with their subordinates. The superintendent, in most cases, does not have this type of contact with his or her principals. Principals are located in their own buildings, and have only occasional face-to-face meetings with the superintendent. A superintendent may have the opportunity to see a principal in direct action as few as four times in an academic year. This low figure is especially true in large, urban districts where there may be as many as fifty principals in a thirty-mile radius. In light of this reality, there must be a great deal of trust established between the two individuals that each is doing his or her job in the most professional way possible.

Developing a true learning organization takes time and commitment. Learning and leading together can create a powerful model for the entire system to embrace. This model of teacher-learner can be then transferred to the schoolhouse as the principal works with his or her teachers and staff.

Senge identifies three critical areas of skills (disciplines) needed in a learning organization: building a shared vision, surfacing and challenging mental models, and engaging in systems thinking. He argues that widespread understanding of these disciplines is required for fostering leadership development across an organization. For our purposes, let us look at Senge's requirements for building a shared vision. He asserts that there are five activities needed to realize an organizational vision:

1. Encouraging personal vision
2. Communicating and asking for support
3. Visioning as an ongoing process
4. Building extrinsic and intrinsic visions
5. Distinguishing positive from negative visions

I want to add one more that is perhaps even more important: the establishment of a two-way communication line before the school year even begins. This communication should have both formal and informal possibilities. Formal communication may be the development of a school improvement plan, a scheduled site visit, an evaluation, or a principal's meeting that the superintendent attends. Informal communication may be through phone discussions, e-mail, unscheduled meetings, site visits, or even a journal dialogue (Diakiw and Beatty, 1991). Regardless of the format, the communication must be such that both the superintendent and the principal feel secure to share successes and concerns.

According to Osborne, "Both the superintendency and the principalship are stressful positions. They are thankless jobs that create a sense of alienation and loneliness. Both are capable of exacting a great personal toll on an individual" (1996, p. 29). Osborne is a Kentucky educator who has worn both hats, superintendent and principal, and has respect for each position. The loneliness of educational administration positions can cause one to lose appreciation for the difficulties of being a superintendent or a principal. It then seems important that neither individual lose perspective on the problems (and joys) inherent in each position.

As instructional leaders, superintendents and principals should have a shared vision for student learning. It is imperative that principals believe in the goals and mission developed for the district as a whole and how they apply to each individual school. Likewise, the superintendent must offer the support and guidance necessary for each principal to create a culture in which every child can achieve these goals.

## *Conclusion*

Although each superintendent-principal dyad is unique, there are certain factors that should be taken into account when developing the relationship. In these times of diminishing resources, increased accountability for outcomes, and demands for educational reform, superintendents and principals must work together in the interest of the success of all children. After all is said and done, superintendents and principals must remember what they have in common: they are both teachers.

## *References*

Bolman, L., and Deal, T. *Reframing Organizations: Artistry, Choice, and Leadership*, 2nd ed. San Francisco: Jossey-Bass, 1997.

Cuban, L. "The Superintendent Contradiction." *Education Week*, Oct. 14, 1998.

Deal, T. E., and Peterson, K. D. *The Leadership Paradox: Balancing Logic and Artistry in Schools.* San Francisco: Jossey-Bass, 1994.

Diakiw, J., and Beatty, N. "A Superintendent and a Principal Write to Each Other." *Educational Leadership*, 1991, *48* (6), 47–50.

Hayden, R. N. "Principal Belief Systems: One Cultural Characteristic Allowing Effective Instructional Leadership." Paper presented at the annual meeting of the American Educational Research Association, Boston, Apr. 1990.

Johnson, S. M. *Leading to Change: The Challenge of the New Superintendency.* San Francisco: Jossey-Bass, 1996.

Osborne, A. "Why I Left the Superintendency for a Principalship." *School Administrator*, 1996, *53* (3), 29–30.

Senge, P. M. "The Leader's New Work: Building Learning Organizations." *Sloan Management Review*, 1990, *32* (1), 7–23.

BOBBIE D'ALESSANDRO *is superintendent of the Cambridge public schools in Cambridge, Massachusetts.*

*Using the metaphor "the Greatest Show on Earth," the author explores ways in which a reciprocal relationship between the superintendent and the principal can lead to school reform. The author mines the complexities in the relationship and reveals their manifestation in mutual admiration, respect for individual achievement and will, support, the creation of a shared vision, and a sense of fun.*

# 10

# The superintendent and the principal: Partners in the "greatest show on earth"

*Lisa Devlin Bjork*

SINCE THE 1983 publication of *A Nation at Risk*, Americans have sustained an intense level of interest in the reform of public education. In this caldron of external scrutiny and internal change, leadership by superintendents and building principals is a critical factor in ensuring that meaningful and lasting change occurs in our schools. As a way of understanding the interconnectedness of these two high-profile positions, I will explore my own experience of the relationship between the superintendent and the principal through the use of a metaphor, the Greatest Show on Earth.

While this phrase typically designates a circus, but is used here with reference to education, I have no intention to demean education. Our

NEW DIRECTIONS FOR SCHOOL LEADERSHIP, NO. 10, WINTER 1998 © JOSSEY-BASS PUBLISHERS

purpose is to educate all students, regardless of race, culture, or economic status, so that they become successful contributors in society. There is nothing "greater" nor more important than achieving that goal. As a metaphor, however, the various acts and performers in the Greatest Show on Earth provide a rich understanding of the complexity that surrounds the fundamental relationships of the designated leaders of the school organization: the superintendent, who is a "leader among leaders" and the principal, who is also a "leader among leaders"—the classroom teachers. Additionally, the Greatest Show occurs in a large, public arena with many events taking place simultaneously. There are clearly demands for each act to be autonomous and highly competent, but still connected to the whole, much like the widely described "loosely coupled" schools with their central office and individual buildings.

In our schools, the key players for achieving success for all students are those most directly involved: the teachers who teach and the principals who lead those teachers. As a superintendent of a mid-sized, Washington State K–12 school district, I work closely with principals in five buildings. Our setting is unique because we are situated on a large island in Puget Sound. We also experience strong community support and examination from a heterogeneous population: wealthy retirees, Boeing commuters, cottage artists, and tradespeople. Our broad political spectrum is demonstrated by some of our local institutions: a retreat center for New Age thinkers; a women writers' center, the Giraffe Project; a Buddhist seminary; and a burgeoning array of fundamentalist Christian churches and schools.

From a superintendent's perspective, the challenge in this district, as in those larger and smaller, is to help create a shared district vision around important issues of school improvement while inviting the principals and staffs to create unique missions at each school site. The result is a balancing act between top-down district-mandated change and building-based initiatives toward reform. As Michael Fullan observes in *Change Forces*, "The centre and local units need each other. You can't get anywhere swinging from one dominance to another. . . . It amounts to simultaneous top-down and bottom-up influence" (1993, p. 38). Neither role can be successful without the cooperation of the other. When both superintendent and principal are wise, they seek ways to leverage the potential power of "top-down" and "bottom-up" working together.

In this two-way relationship between the district superintendent and the building principals, there are five critical elements for creating and maintaining successful relationships: (1) establishment of trust; (2) recognition of and support for facing significant issues; (3) commitment to a common vision and direction while honoring autonomy; (4) promotion and advocacy of each other's work; and (5) support, relaxation, and fun.

## *The Trapeze Act: Establishment of Trust*

Foundational to any other aspect of the relationship is the creation of a trusting relationship between the superintendent and the principal. Within the Greatest Show on Earth, "the trapeze act" is an apt metaphor to describe the critical place of trust in a relationship between the superintendent and the principal. Trapeze artists fling themselves into space, stretching out, and risking all, with the belief that they will be caught by the person hanging from the other trapeze. Often we administrators feel like we are stepping out into empty space, particularly as we embark on a new area of school reform.

In the past five years in our district, individual schools have implemented a high school block schedule, a middle school staff teaming model, and an elementary school integrated, thematic curriculum. In all instances, there was a predictable period of anxiety and stress for staff and parents as they went through a transition to the innovation. The principals' willingness to move ahead in flinging themselves through the empty space that surrounds an innovation came from a confidence, a trust, that they would be caught, and that there would be a safety net for them in case of an occasional slip. When there is public outcry, the superintendent can provide equally public responses of support. Privately, there can be conversations concerning strategy and approach. Fundamentally, however, success is based on mutual trust and a high degree of competence by each individual. Trust stems from an honest commitment by the superintendent to an agreed-upon action that is not aborted by external pressures.

At the district level, we instituted a mandatory writing assessment at grades 2, 5, 8, and 10 that included a graduation requirement. Because this "district" initiative actually came about as an outgrowth of teacher curriculum work, a principal/site council initiative, and consensus by the entire administrative team, it was never seen as a top-down imposition. In the instance described above, the reciprocal relationship created a synergy greater than any one group acting alone. At times, one artist is the leader or initiator; at other times, it is another.

Sometimes the trapeze artists don't quite connect with each other; their timing is off. Perhaps, as in schools, they were preoccupied momentarily with other things. Within the school system, we jokingly describe trust as "no surprises." In real terms, the superintendent hates to get a call from a board of directors member inquiring: "Dr. Bjork, why didn't the principal discipline that student who painted graffiti on the wall of the school last week? He's still in school, and I understand he is still playing football." While mumbling my response and promising to get information back to the board member, I remember that there is always another explanation. And there is. So, even though I missed having the information prior to the phone call, a foundation of trust tempers my response to the principal. We can climb out of the safety net, return to the trapeze, and continue our performance.

## The Lion Tamer: Recognition of and Support for Facing Critical Issues

There are those who say "Problems are our friends," that problems are an integral part of meaningful change. Whether they are "friendly" is debatable, but problems are definitely part of the fabric of life in schools. At both the building and the district levels, we must learn to first recognize, then understand, and finally confront problems with creativity and courage. While the superintendent has a critical role in both modeling this behavior and in establishing an atmosphere of trust in which problems can be raised and discussed openly, anyone can take a turn at "taming the lion."

For example, a principal may tell me that he senses a growing unrest among the parents of "gifted children." The issue seems larger than a single grade level or school. As we clarify who the lion is and what its behavioral characteristics might be, we are also brainstorming about who in the district might best suit the role of tamer. In this instance, the lion tamer is the assistant superintendent who gathers parents and staff together to problem-solve.

Sometimes, an issue comes to my attention through community or staff contact. A recent example is a concern for school safety, which has been part of the national agenda and now surfaces locally in such places as teacher association negotiations, bus driver concerns, parent telephone calls, and board meetings. This appears to be a large lion. With the assistance of the principals and others in the district, I attempt to walk around the lion and understand his characteristics before moving too far in one direction or another. I am proactive in creating sufficient support for myself and for the principal who may in the future have to face the lion alone with only a metaphorical chair and whip. I do this through writing procedure and working with the community.

The principal may encounter a parent at a PTSA meeting who asks: "Are my children safe at your school?" With the district and building review complete, the principal has good information to share with the parent, as do I if I receive a similar question from community members. We are working together clarifying and describing problems, deciding on a process for dealing with them, providing support tools, and selecting the best person for lion tamer.

---

## The Horseback Riders: Individuality and Commitment to a Common Vision

Watch the amazing feats of those who ride horseback. They jump on and off the backs of the running horses with great dexterity, grace, and balance. This is like the work of superintendents and principals in that there is constant movement and activity, a demand for flexibility, and decision making of small and large import. Moreover, we often feel as if we are running in circles.

Certainly, all the members of this act must be going in the same direction with a delight in their individual artistry, color, and movement. Similarly, relationships vary between superintendent and individual principals. There is no "one size fits all" here. As a frequent visitor to each school, I am aware of principals' challenges and successes in their buildings. I am also knowledgeable about the strengths principals bring to their positions, and where they might need support or guidance. Flexibility is a required ingredient if I am to respond differently to individuals based on their experience, personal and professional needs, personality, current school status, and gender.

With a first-year principal who has had no previous experience as a building principal, my role is much more being the guide and mentor. I am careful to make sure that the principal gains the knowledge needed, but also has a nonjudgmental ear to listen to observations and questions about staff. For example, if the principal is concerned about a particular grade level of staff or how to operate a site council, the superintendent needs to listen, understand, and then ask questions to help the principal clarify his or her own understanding of the situation.

Certainly another variable is that of gender. As a woman superintendent who supervises both male and female principals, I do factor into the relationship special opportunities that stem from cross- or same-gender relationships. However, in my particular situation, this factor seems far less important than variables of personality, experience, and leadership styles. I have worked with three male principals and two male assistant principals, and each seems to have different leadership strengths that we build on together. Communication with all five also varies depending upon their particular styles and my interactions with them. For example, one tends to be more philosophical and general as he considers the implications and ambiguities of a situation, while a different principal is more concrete-sequential in his approach.

The four women administrators have varying degrees of experience and talents, and so my relationship with each is slightly different. No one in either gender group displays only stereotypically male or female characteristics, and neither do I. For instance, all the principals with whom I work have their egos connected to their school's performance, and all exhibit caring toward their staff and students. Perhaps it is that the leadership roles, all of which had been historically fashioned in the image of men, have facilitated women administrators' ability to be more assertive. Likewise, the men who come up through the teaching profession, which is still female-dominated and female-normed, have had the benefit of becoming more nurturing and caring individuals at the workplace.

It is important to always build on the strength of the individual. With confidence in their own strength and abilities, principals will have the courage to risk the jump to the back of the horse, but even more important, the task of creating their own beautiful performance while going around the ring at high speed.

Along with the encouragement of strong autonomous principals, there exists the seemingly contradictory challenge of forging a central district vision that keeps us all running around the ring in the same direction so that we don't bump into each other. Susan More Johnson (1996) describes a variety of approaches leading to different outcomes used by superintendents as they conduct districtwide strategic planning processes. From my experience, creation of a common vision happens best when it occurs over time and is embraced, even discovered, by those who must implement it. Thus, my role is to create an inclusive process that gathers up the best dreams that exist throughout the schools and community. Then, with the help of others, we consolidate these beliefs into a central vision that is communicated back to the principals and staffs. Ideally, they can recognize their own best dreams embedded in the district plan. This is a critical example of the central task of respecting individual autonomy, responding flexibly, and creating a broad district vision.

## The Ringmaster: Promotion and Advocacy of Each Others' Work

Traditionally, the role of superintendent most closely resembles that of the ringmaster. As the positional head of the organization, the superintendent is seen as the person in charge, the public spokesperson, the one who organizes everyone else—and perhaps tells them what to do. However, as we know from research and our own commonsense understanding of teaching and learning, it is in schools and classrooms where the critical interactions occur.

While the superintendent as figurehead is often in the "center ring" of public gatherings, there is much more to this role than would appear on the surface. If the ringmaster blows the whistle, announces an act, and no act appears, the ringmaster is left standing alone in front of the audience. This illustrates the critical importance of the principal as the prime mover and developer of his or her own school or "act." In this regard, the ringmaster is merely the announcer and promoter of the work that is going on within the schools. The job is to advocate for and celebrate the hard work being done behind the scenes until it can be "rolled out" for public consumption.

In this period of intense public criticism of schools, it is more important than ever for superintendents to seek ways in which to reward and recognize the work of the principal. The recognition can occur privately, or in front of peers. Recognition can occur at board meetings or at parent groups. But its value cannot be underestimated.

Another twist on the metaphor is to understand that at any given time a principal may step in as ringmaster. There are times when a particular principal has expertise and understanding of a situation or program from which the superintendent can draw. For example, as we move to an elementary reading accountability system in Washington State, it is the elementary principals who lead us forward through their own staff collaboration and development of an improvement plan. When the principals present the plan to the board, they are seen as highly competent professionals who have the knowledge and wisdom to lead the district forward. To appear publicly in a position of district leadership provides another type of authentic recognition.

Informally in conversations with teachers and parents, and formally at faculty meetings or parent meetings, the principal can also help explain and support the work of the superintendent. If the principals are informed colleagues who are knowledgeable about the district's decisions, then they can more naturally support the district initiatives—thereby becoming ringmasters themselves. This aspect of advocacy is really dependent on the relationship described earlier that is based on trust and respect for each individual in creating a common vision that reflects the spirit of the entire district.

## *Send in the Clowns: Mutual Support, Relaxation, and Fun*

A superintendent's role that is often overlooked is that of creating a relaxed sense of fun—because we know that workers do best in a state of "flow," often at odds with the hectic and varied pace of both the building principal and the superintendent. When we meet as a group, the superintendent has a definite role in creating an atmosphere of mutual support and fun that can carry the individuals back into their workplace refreshed. We also schedule time for fun during retreats or conferences—just being together builds a foundation of trust and rapport that can carry over into times of hard decisions or scarce resources. If we are able to help each other express our enjoyment and relaxation, then we can communicate positively to others in the "audience," most particularly students, their parents, and staff.

Individually, there are both public and private opportunities for support. Drop-in visits to a principal's office on a day when there has been a crisis, or during a time of conflict with staff or parents, gives us both the opportunity to listen and think-through situations. An occasional lunch "down town" with the superintendent can help the principal relax and expand in a nonwork setting. Overall, the intent is to bring each other humor and relaxation within the context of our very demanding jobs.

## *Conclusion*

As illuminated by a comparison to the Greatest Show on Earth, the critical relationship between the superintendent and the principal is characterized by complexity and reciprocity. Both educators work as leaders in very public settings observed by several audiences. Sometimes superintendents and principals perform together—connected by the trust that marks the trapeze act; and sometimes they perform alone—like the lion tamer confronting the lion. However, even when acting alone, mutual support is necessary to understand and face the current problem. An appreciation of the horseback riders helps us glimpse the paradoxical importance of autonomy and unanimity in order to create a common district direction. As ringmasters, an appreciation of district efforts must be promoted loudly in the various circles open to the superintendent and the principal in order for the good work to continue. Finally, the clowns are sent in to remind us that support, relaxation, and fun are critical to establishing an environment in which principals and superintendents are able to reach their potential.

Together the various acts of the Greatest Show on Earth, when applied to the school setting, strongly suggest that trust is foundational to the creation of dynamic and reciprocal relationships between the superintendent and the principals. With strong relationships between the district and building leaders, schools can change in ways that are both meaningful to students and respectful of the professionals implementing the reforms.

### References

Fullan, M. *Change Forces: Probing the Depths of Educational Reform.* Bristol, Pa.: Falmer Press, 1993.
Johnson, S. M. *Leading to Change: The Challenge of the New Superintendency.* San Francisco: Jossey-Bass, 1996.

LISA DEVLIN BJORK *is superintendent of the South Whidbey school district in Washington State.*

*The author offers an unusual framework for thinking about the principal-superintendent relationship: he likens administrative challenges to the risks taken and lessons learned by Washington State eighth graders as they sail the San Juan Islands. It takes the passion of the open seas for this principal to adequately provide a parallel emotional and learning experience to that of educational leadership.*

# 11

# Button down the mainsail

*Greg Willis*

AS SCHOOLS CONTINUE their efforts to become truly collaborative communities, the roles and responsibilities of all participants are in a state of constant change. In these times of rapid and complex change, it is important for leaders to slow down and take the time to reflect. Reflecting on the way we have done things in the past can help us break patterns and find alternate paths. Reflection also offers opportunities for affirmation and renewal. As learners ourselves we have much to gain from looking closely at our students and teachers. My purpose is to share reflections of a single program in our school, in an attempt to shed light on "what matters" in the work the superintendent and principal do.

NEW DIRECTIONS FOR SCHOOL LEADERSHIP, NO. 10, WINTER 1998 © JOSSEY-BASS PUBLISHERS

## *Imagine*

Imagine the pure exhilaration and satisfaction as the last member of the group makes it over a ten-foot wall in a cooperative, problem-solving experience at the Ropes Course. Imagine fists raised in the air, shouts of accomplishment, and the emerging sense that we're all in this together. Imagine kneeling on the deck of a fifty-foot ketch, straining shoulder to shoulder with students to button down a mainsail cover in preparation for our first landing, after the four-hour sail across the Sound. Imagine watching the faces of thirty students as they sit in a circle in the tribal longhouse, listening intently to an elder of the Swinomish tribe, mesmerized as he shares his stories, culture, beliefs, and most important, himself. Imagine sitting in a gymnasium with six hundred middle school students and staff as the students of the Sailing Expedition flash their slide show onto the high wall. In the background a group of student musicians and the chorus perform an original song written by one of the student musicians. Six hundred eleven- to fourteen-year-olds are held in awe by the sheer power and beauty of the experience.

These images are just four brief moments in a five-day journey of personal discovery and growth. Each year, two groups of our eighth graders journey into the San Juan Islands for sailing and adventure. This truly unique and rich learning opportunity provides a revealing glimpse into the core values and conditions under which students and staff thrive. For me, any discussion about education must always begin and end with students. While making the connection between the sailing expedition and what the superintendent and principal should consider in their roles as leaders may take a leap of faith, those involved in the enterprise of teaching and learning will relate to the title of the program in which this journey takes place, "Adventure Education."

## *The Vision*

As with any meaningful and worthwhile learning experience, the program started with the idea of one or a small group of people. In this case, it was two young teachers with a passion for sailing and the sea. Not surprisingly, when they first proposed taking middle school students to sea they encountered myriad obstacles, resistance, and questions. The very first attempt came during an enrichment session and involved taking seven students sailing out in the local harbor. When they returned three hours later, the excitement and exhilaration in their eyes and voices was beyond description. The door had been opened and the exploration had begun. It was an important moment, both in terms of our program and our approach. Five years later, the program is fully in place and expanding. It began with a vision, fueled by a passion and founded on the belief that there was another way to teach kids. Like so many innovations or initiatives in schools, the task seemed daunting. Anytime we head into the unknown there is a certain amount of apprehension. Often the first step or two is the key—in this case, without taking that first jaunt into the harbor, the opportunity would have been lost.

Parallel: The superintendent and principal must model and promote the value of openness in their leadership. We must invite ideas, participation, and diversity, and we must encourage innovation and initiatives. Believing in people, in their desire and capacity to do good work and their will to constantly improve, is a necessary starting place. Securing and providing resources, whether in the form of fiscal support, time, or personnel, reinforces such an invitation. To gain real commitment, not mere compliance, to a shared vision, people must have the opportunity to help create that vision. Creating opportunities for people to contribute in meaningful ways allows them to feel connected. Leadership emerges from all directions and builds upon itself. As we develop a sense of belonging and collective purpose, the potential for change is unlocked. Understanding the willingness and ability levels of people has always been important. Recognizing their passions and letting them run with their dreams is a motivating force. There seems little question that creating a healthy workplace and life for teachers has a positive effect on the quality of schooling for students.

## Discovering Purpose

At the heart of the program is the belief that young people have incredible talents and capacities, and, given the right opportunities, can and will rise to the occasion. Secondly, learning takes place in a variety of settings and that experiential education is a powerful tool. From the beginning, our students were responsible for planning and carrying out every aspect of the trip. They wrote letters, set schedules, made docking and camping arrangements, organized food and menus, and gathered the necessary gear and equipment. These responsibilities, often new for many of our students, helped create a sense of importance. They realize very quickly that the success of their adventure is dependent on their involvement, hard work, and willingness to share the load. Being entrusted with meaningful roles is motivating, no matter what the age. Participating in decisions that affect us and those around us creates a feeling of contribution. Working in cooperation and achieving a common goal reveals the power of collective effort. These early tasks promote a sense of value and competence and teach the youngsters that they are contributing to something larger than themselves.

Parallel: The heart of our enterprise is a love for kids and a genuine concern about their welfare now and in the future. Students are the driving force behind everything we do. Thus it is incumbent on the superintendent and the principal to model this value through words and action. Be visible: attend and participate in student activities. In all discussions and decisions, always come back to the question, "What's best for the kids?" Create student recognition activities for all different types and levels of contribution. Help students engage directly in the community through apprenticeships and service. Take every opportunity to talk about students, both inside the district and in the larger community.

## Setting the Stage

The planning and preparation stage takes five to six weeks and requires hard work and commitment from all the players. Throughout this period, they are also involved with the learning that is pre-requisite for the trip. Our captains come in and teach lessons on sailing, procedures, and general navigation. The Coast Guard presents lessons on safety and the geography of the region. Representatives of the state park service discuss the plant and animal ecology of the surrounding islands and waters. It is an intense time with much expected and gained. By the day of departure, the students have invested themselves deeply in the learning and doing process. Excitement and confidence gradually build, yet there is still a sense of the unknown. Even though the direction has been set and the contingency plans are in place, there are variables beyond control.

Parallel: We expend amazing amounts of time, energy, and commitment in planning and preparation. The superintendent and the principal need to guide the process for selecting initiatives for change carefully. Proposals must align with the stated vision and plan in the district. The Sailing Expedition, for example, fit perfectly into the part of our district's strategic plan calling for the utilization of flexible learning environments. The frequency and timing of proposed changes should be considered. The constant bombardment of change can keep us off balance and have disastrous effects. Controlling the rate may be less difficult for the principal because those initiatives generated within the building often have strong support. The superintendent, on the other hand, often deals with initiatives from the outside. Whichever the case, it is imperative that we filter these changes in a realistic and manageable way. Often the planning stage involves widespread participation, cooperation, discussion, and anticipation. These activities bring excitement and enthusiasm, but also a similar sense of heading into the unknown. We can minimize the unknown by anticipating problems and designing alternatives. The confidence we build each time we are successful helps to overcome the hesitation.

## Breaking Away

The first day of the expedition sets the tone for everything to follow. The morning begins with a trip to the Ropes Course, which builds confidence, cooperation, and communication. Throughout this first day the importance of listening is the central theme. Given the nature of the high-ropes exercise and sailing on a fifty-two-foot sailboat in the middle of Puget Sound, the importance of listening takes on new meaning. Skills in problem solving, communicating, and working together are reinforced at every turn. Following the Ropes Course, the students travel to the dock and then unload and store all their equipment, food, and clothing. At this point, the captain's meeting focuses on communication, cooperation, and listening. The moment arrives and the students, staff, and volunteers set sail and the adventure begins. As with any new experience, there is a settling-in period, and the first day on the water allows the crew to find their sea legs and balance. The preparation and abstract discussions become real and connections begin to be made. Once under way, students begin to apply the skills they learned prior to departure. They are organized into smaller watch groups and rotate responsibilities every half hour. They take turns at the wheel, setting sails, charting the course, logging the passage, and (the favorite) out on the front keeping an eye to the horizon. This sharing and experiencing of all the different responsibilities provides an early understanding of what it takes to sail and reach destination.

Parallel: Effective leadership requires well-developed communication skills. Without the ability to listen, there is no communication. Listening conveys respect and builds trust. The superintendent and the principal need to listen closely to those around them—including each other. An open, continuous, and honest dialogue is required to bring about substantial change.

## The Heartland

The first stop on the journey offers the crew a unique and memorable opportunity. The evening is spent in LaConner at the Swinomish Tribal Center, meeting and sharing a meal with members of the community. Several of the elders talk and share their wisdom and culture with our students. They speak from the heart and always with great respect for the surrounding waters and mountains. They share their beliefs and traditions and always express a spirit of welcomeness. The importance of the lesson of the day, listening, comes home immediately. Members of the tribe play music and everyone gets involved in the circle dance that is a custom. In the end everyone retires to find their place for the night, exhausted by the effort and excitement of the day, and satisfied in the knowledge that they turned what once seemed a dream into a reality. The emerging realization of what they had and were accomplishing begins to grow. And this is just the first day!

Parallel: Effective leaders lead with their heart, as well as with their head. The expression of feelings as well as ideas is healthy. Expanding our circle of influence, meeting new people, and learning their ways facilitates personal and professional growth. The ability to establish and maintain relationships should not be underestimated.

## Building Connections

From the outset the staff intended to integrate as many subject areas as possible into the experience. The ability to apply knowledge comes from the connections we are able to make between the things we learn. The history, geography, and ecology of the region provide the background. The teachers and captains add applications for math, writing, art, marine science, and technology. Skills in communication, problem solving, cooperation, and decision making are utilized and practiced at every opportunity. There is a wholeness to the experience that adds depth and meaning. Could it be that there is a bridge between this type of curriculum integration in real-life situations and the development of the fully integrated person?

Parallel: The effective integration of curriculum builds connection and meaning for students. An organization that builds bridges between teachers, schools, and the district has the same potential. Like subject areas, these three groups are interdependent. Collaboration can and should extend beyond the building. Opportunities for discussion between schools, focused on real issues, has potential to build a cooperative venture. Meetings and discussions alone, however, don't reach that level of "walk in my shoes" understanding that it sometimes takes to truly empathize with a colleague. Like life on the sailboat, rotating and exchanging responsibilities builds understanding and appreciation. At the building level, we can extend invitations and create opportunities for central office staff to interact with students and staff. As principal I need to identify and support leadership opportunities for every staff member. A large part of our success as a school has been the incredible leadership our staff has shown.

---

## In the Neighborhood

We continue to grow in our recognition of the importance of our connection to the local community. The support and resources available to us and the willingness of people to get involved add a powerful dimension. The sailing expedition exemplifies this potential. The captains of our boats have always donated their time, ships, and expertise to the program. They share their passion and love of sailing with everyone involved. The spirit of giving as well as their patience and teaching ability serve as models to all of us. Likewise, the parent volunteers model and contribute to the sense of community that develops during the five days. The interactions between and among these groups promotes understanding and respect.

Parallel: Encourage widespread activities for parents and community to interact directly with the schools. Participation in activities like service projects, the Science Olympiad, special event nights, and programs like the sailing trip build understanding and appreciation. PTSA and site council participation are vehicles for much-needed work and representation. At the district level, participation in strategic planning and other planning committees provides valuable input. If a school is truly to be a community, it must include and embrace the community beyond its walls.

## Onward

A major factor in the success of the Adventure Education program has been its ability to evolve and grow over time. The creative impulse of the staff has allowed for expansion of the program at every turn. For example, the addition of a kayaking station off one of the islands allows students to learn to navigate their own vessels. A dedicated group of AmeriCorp volunteers work in our district each year modeling the value of service. This past year, the entire group not only participated, but sailed their own boat alongside ours. Their involvement has expanded the circle of significant adults working with our young people—to the benefit of all. On each trip one or two former students return and assist the staff and students. This cross-age opportunity builds natural bridges between us and the high school.

Last fall, a new dimension was added. Students were required to design methods of communicating their experience to others. In small groups, they developed a slide show, a radio program, a web page, a song, and a video. The concluding activity was a presentation to the entire student body. This drive to extend learning is ever-present and often results in the blossoming of a passion for a specific area or skill. Students accompany the team to present at regional conferences. Additional staff members are invited on each voyage. All of these changes reflect the strong commitment and dedication of the three teachers now at the lead. They give their time, energy, and expertise unselfishly. Despite the program's recognized success, they continually seek ways to make the program better.

Parallel: The superintendent and the principal must encourage and expect continuous improvement. Along with this expectation comes the responsibility to support such improvement, whether with fiscal assistance, time, or personnel. We must be willing to problem-solve, lend a hand, and follow through. The Adventure Education program has met and overcome many obstacles and setbacks over the years. A leader must be willing to struggle through the hard times as well as the good times. Our own drive toward growth and improvement must be clear. There must be an ongoing assessment of progress toward our purpose and vision.

---

## Looking Inward

Reflection time is an aspect of the experience that is built in and expected. Throughout the trip, students are provided opportunities to spend time by themselves. The purpose of this quiet time is to reflect on the experience, to think about what's been learned, and to ponder how the learning applies in a larger sense. Putting these reflections on paper is part of the integrated nature of the program. A time is provided to share these thoughts and feelings with the larger group during the campfire on the final night. For many of the students this reflection time may be the first time they have ever spent with themselves in a natural setting. The experience of publicly sharing their inner thoughts can also be a new experience. Although no one is required to share, most seem to want to share what has been awakened.

Parallel: Reflection is a powerful tool for change and growth. Reflecting on the old ways of doing business can help us break familiar patterns and find new ways. Reflection can also be reinforcing and renewing. Teachers and administrators need time to reflect on the work they do, and opportunities for sharing these reflections with their peers. Superintendents and principals also need time together to reflect and openly explore. Discussions of the things that "really matter" will emerge.

---

## Learning from Each Other

Staff development is a critical element in building a culture of school improvement. While we continue to seek and develop opportunities for staff to grow, many of our attempts have fallen short. Developing activities that focus on ideas or strategies that connect with what actually transpires between students and teachers is the key. In an attempt to better understand curriculum integration we designed a staff development activity around the sailing expedition. Six of our teachers developed minilessons around the topic of sailing. The day included a large-group trust-building activity; small-group lessons in navigation, art, poetry, and technology; and three hours on the boat learning the same lessons and responsibilities as our students during the actual trip. In addition, we all shared a lunch together and at the end of the day held an evaluation and feedback session. The reflections and comments during the last session were exceedingly positive. "The best staff development activity I've ever attended" seemed to be the note of the day. It was a productive and memorable experience and it was fun!

Parallel: We are surrounded by talented, experienced, and creative people. They have credibility and much to offer in the way of ideas and expertise. Their knowledge of the people and dynamics provide context. We need to look more often to the inside for ideas and solutions. Staff development that is ongoing, integrated, locally designed, and practical has the greatest potential for connecting people's hearts and minds with the things that really matter. And yes, learning can be fun.

## Cloudy Weather

There have been times along the way when conditions affected the smooth sailing that has generally been our good fortune. One spring, the expedition ran into high winds and abnormally hard rain on the second day. The skippers and crew followed their contingency plans and headed for a safe harbor. Try as they might for the next couple of days, and they tried mightily, to keep up morale, the trip was forced to end a day early. Students and staff took ferries and then boarded buses for home. There was great disappointment, and yet many beneficial lessons learned. Adversity can be a learning experience.

Parallel: No matter how well we plan or what contingencies we develop, there will be times when forces beyond our control may bring disappointment. Likewise, we will make mistakes. If we do, we need to acknowledge them and apply what we've learned. In a culture where mistakes are allowed, we can free people up to explore and innovate.

## *Jubilation*

There is a moment near the end of each adventure that every participant will remember. Sailing under the bridge at Deception Pass marks the final turn home. There is celebration in that moment— a sense of accomplishment, personal discovery, and independence. We feel that we can, both individually and collectively, achieve anything we set our hearts and minds to. More than confidence, there is a sense of hope. Is there anything more powerful?

Parallel: The superintendent and the principal can and should strive, through words and deeds, to recognize, appreciate, and celebrate contributions—the talents, efforts, and courage that students demonstrate everyday; the creative energy and leadership of staff; and the support of volunteers. Establish a rhythm that allows for slowing down, appreciating the moment, looking into the eyes of another, seeing a spark, and making contact. It is in these moments that we find purpose and inspiration. Make experiencing joy a worthwhile and expressed norm. Be awed by the capacities of those around you. To translate the collaborative process into gains in student learning, we must take the process to the next level. It is in an environment of hope, inspiration, and joy that we may generate the belief and passion for such an endeavor.

## *Coming Home*

At that point, hearts turn homeward. No matter how stimulating and fun an experience, there is comfort and excitement in heading for home. Whether returning from an overnight trip, a two-week holiday, or just a day at school or work, there is joy in knowing that soon we will be back with those who love us most. For some of our students, this is the first extended time away from home and the strength of this feeling is a lesson in and of itself.

Parallel: Go home, spend time with the ones you love, and relax. Good health, both physical and mental, is necessary to generate the strength and endurance required of every person in the school system. We have come a long way, but there's still work to do.

GREG WILLIS *is principal of the Langley Middle School on South Whidbey Island in Washington State.*

# Index

# Back Issue/Subscription Order Form

Copy or detach and send to:
**Jossey-Bass Inc., Publishers, 350 Sansome Street, San Francisco CA 94104-1342**

Call or fax toll free!
**Phone 888-378-2537 6AM-5PM PST; Fax 800-605-2665**

Back issues: Please send me the following issues at $25 each.
(Important: please include series initials and issue number, such as SL8.)

1. SL _____

_____

_____

$ _____ Total for single issues

$ _____ Shipping charges (for single issues *only;* subscriptions are exempt from shipping charges): Up to $30, add $5$^{50}$ • $30$^{01}$–$50, add $6$^{50}$ $50$^{01}$–$75, add $7$^{50}$ • $75$^{01}$–$100, add $9 • $100$^{01}$–$150, add $10 Over $150, call for shipping charge.

Subscriptions Please ❑ start   ❑ renew my subscription to *New Directions for School Leadership* for the year 19\_\_\_ at the following rate:

❑ Individual $52     ❑ Institutional $105
**NOTE:** Subscriptions are quarterly, and are for the calendar year only. Subscriptions begin with the spring issue of the year indicated above. For shipping outside the U.S., please add $25.

$ _____ Total single issues and subscriptions (CA, IN, NJ, NY and DC residents, add sales tax for single issues. NY and DC residents must include shipping charges when calculating sales tax. NY and Canadian residents only, add sales tax for subscriptions.)

❑ Payment enclosed (U.S. check or money order only)
❑ VISA, MC, AmEx, Discover Card #_____ Exp. date_____

Signature _____ Day phone _____
❑ Bill me (U.S. institutional orders only. Purchase order required.)
Purchase order #_____

Name _____
Address _____

_____

Phone_____ E-mail _____

For more information about Jossey-Bass Publishers, visit our Web site at:
www.josseybass.com                    **PRIORITY CODE = ND1**